By the same author

Il Colore del Vento
African Nights
I Dreamed of Africa

Night of the Lions

Kuki Gallmann

VIKING

For Makena, a daughter of Africa, and for
all my young African friends

VIKING

Published by the Penguin Group
Penguin Books Ltd, 27 Wrights Lane, London w8 5TZ, England
Penguin Putnam Inc., 375 Hudson Street, New York, New York 10014, USA
Penguin Books Australia Ltd, Ringwood, Victoria, Australia
Penguin Books Canada Ltd, 10 Alcorn Avenue, Toronto, Ontario, Canada M4V 3B2
Penguin Books (NZ) Ltd, Private Bag 102902, NSMC, Auckland, New Zealand

Penguin Books Ltd, Registered Offices: Harmondsworth, Middlesex, England

First published 1999
1 3 5 7 9 10 8 6 4 2

Set in 12.5/15pt Monotype Fournier
Typeset by Rowland Phototypesetting Ltd, Bury St Edmunds, Suffolk
Printed in England by Clays Ltd, St Ives plc

A CIP catalogue record for this book is available from the British Library

ISBN 0-670-88310-7

Dreams can change your life, and eventually the world.

FATIMA MERNISSI, *The Harem Within*

Contents

CONTENTS

PART TWO
Only Dust, at Arba Jahan

List of Illustrations

ETHIOPIA

Moyale

BORAN

MOYALE

Fujiyanyota
(Start of the Trek)

BORAN

Dololo Chaka

Dida Galgalo
Desert

Dololo Nure

Laga Mudama

Laga Cholchuff

Garsa

ADJURAN
(SOMALI)

Marsabit

Dololo Barstr
Desert

Arba Jahan

Wagir

Lava plateau

Laisamis

Lava plateau

Barchuma
Bidich

Koiya Wells

RENDILLE

Kairu sand river

Wamba

Lontopi Spring

Il Baaokut

Lolokwe Mountain

SAMBURU

N

Isiolo

THE CAMEL TREK

Mt Kenya

→ Main route 🮲🮳 Mountains

0 10 20 30 40 50 miles
0   50   100 km

Acknowledgements

I would like to thank my African friends at Ol ari Nyiro, for their loyal support, and for holding the fort when I was deep in my writing; my readers, who have taken the time to write that they have fallen in love with Africa by reading my stories, have travelled to Kenya to discover their truth and, having found it, have become the good-will ambassadors this continent needs.

Gilfrid Powys, always; Toby Eady, my 'brother', agent and staunchest ally; Aino Block, who once again enthusiastically read my script; Adrian House, for his advice; the Gallmann Memorial Foundation's patron, team and supporters, for helping the dream. My daughter 'Makena', for her love, her wisdom and her smile.

Introduction

When I first came to Africa, the people addressed me as Memsaab; in time, they baptized me Nyawera, The One Who Works Hard. Now, they call me Mama.

Because I have chosen to stay, and because I belong.

Africa is a continent of extremes.

There is an Africa of tragedy and famine, of corruption and war, of blood and hunger and tears, of incurable disease and tribal clashes and political unrest. There are droughts and there are floods. There are crowded cities, glue-sniffing street children, child-prostitutes, bidonvilles where open sewage carries the lurid refuse of a hopeless conglomerate of people with no jobs, no homes, no future, roads littered with potholes and garbage heaps where skinny goats forage.

It is the Africa one reads about today in every paper, the one we daily see in reports on cable television. It is a captive Africa, dependent on the blackmail of foreign aid, constantly judged, constantly criticized and never understood. Here the rich West has imprinted its competitive, frantic image, created alien needs, imposed alien philosophies and financed impossible schemes, unsuited to the true spirit and potential of this troubled and fantastic continent, all too ready to take back that help and sit in judgement of yet another failure.

I do not sing that Africa.

There is no need for yet another negative reportage, which would leave a bitter taste and would serve no purpose.

There is a different side to this ancient land. It is the Africa that, since the beginning of time, has evoked in travellers a deep recognition, an inexplicable yearning to return. The place which still has what most of the world has lost. Space. Roots. Traditions. Stunning beauty. True wilderness. Rare animals. Extraordinary people. The land that will always attract those who can still dream.

This Africa, into whose embrace went Paolo and Emanuele, called early to the land of beyond, healed my sorrow and became my life purpose. This maternal, primordial Africa taught me acceptance, endurance and survival. I recognized it as a place where wisdom could be found. A place to end this journey, and begin a new one. A place of renewal and rebirth. A good place to die.

In the very heart of Kenya where I still live, Ol ari Nyiro – The Place of Dark Waters – I walked the hills and the valleys in those dark days of solitude, tiring my body, asking the wind the questions whose answers are the reasons for life. I missed Paolo, a man for all seasons and places, handsome, gifted with irresistible charm, eloquent and brave, happy in the bush and at ease in a palace; I missed his poetry and flair. I missed Emanuele, who taught me first what it means to be a mother, my sensitive, intelligent boy, whose eyes had the sadness and wisdom of ages, who was taken into that good night by one of the snakes he had loved.

Walking alone through the pervading magic of untouched

African landscapes, open to growth as one is when at the bottom of pain, I felt quintessentially part of the whole. One evening, looking down at the breathtaking depths of the Mukutan Gorge on the Great Rift Valley, in this living cathedral of the spirit I found peace.

There was Sveva, the daughter Paolo would never know, the radiant girl who was my hope and my future. I was in Africa, and this was my cure.

In memory of Paolo and Emanuele I started the Gallmann Memorial Foundation and devoted the rest of my life to making a positive difference for the African environment.

Mine are love stories about Kenya, my Africa.

It is the Africa of sunshine and breathtaking, endless vistas, of roaming herds on the plains, of red dust and galloping giraffe, of forests and snow and prehistoric lakes, of gentle, handsome, intelligent people whose poverty is not of the spirit. People for whom tradition is important, to whom family values still matter, who protect the young and respect the old, care for the sick and feed the hungry, even if it means sharing the little that they have; generous people, ready to smile, and to forgive; people with a song in their heart and a dance in their step; enduring, compassionate and infinitely patient. The people of Kenya, whose antique, proven wisdom I respect. I salute them and I thank them for having allowed me to live amongst them, to bury my men in the soil of my garden, as Africans do, and for allowing me the honour and the choice of becoming a Kenyan like them.

*

I have new stories to tell. I have old stories that I have not yet told.

The elephant, after dark, raid my garden at Kuti as they did a quarter of a century ago; I encounter – now more than ever – buffalo in my car lights; there are still rhino coming to the salt lick below The Nest, and in the moonless nights lions prey on the cattle around the *boma*, as they have since the beginning of lion and cattle in Africa. Butterflies and rare birds bejewel the forests and on the silent lakes millions of pink flamingo forage.

The Pokot herders stand on one leg, a black blanket thrown over a shoulder with supreme elegance, necks bright with beads and an ostrich feather beckoning on their skull cap.

The waves of another tide reach silently along the mangroves, while the fish eagle surveys her hunting grounds somewhere on the north coast, away from the beaten tracks. There are still remote places untouched by man's progress, where harmony prevails.

Magic, and the inexplicable, still touch our lives. This is the lyrical, therapeutic Africa that I describe; the one I live every day of my life. The one that it is my life aim to preserve.

Scores of bright young Kenyans visit the Wilderness Education Centre, which I built to honour the memory of my son, and discover in Ol ari Nyiro their Africa. Each of these children is a messenger, who will carry this crusade a step further. Through education and experience the generation of today will realize the importance of their unique environment.

For the world needs beauty and youth needs hope.

It is to these young people, and to my daughter Sveva, whom they call Makena, that I dedicate this book of true stories.

PART ONE

Tales of the Great Rift Valley

The Summer of the Crayfish

For my father

Looking on the happy Autumn fields,
And thinking of the days that are no more.

TENNYSON, *The Princess*

On the opposite bank, two camels browsed with prehensile lips from the waxy shrubs of rhus. They moved on phlegmatically and in seconds disappeared completely. Harvester ants busily carried grass seeds, zig-zagging in a scattered procession, hurrying down their holes. Crouched on my haunches, the sun hot on the back of my khaki shirt and on my naked legs, I was fishing.

The brown surface of the water broke in a ripple and a large muddy claw emerged, to grab the morsel of rotten meat tied to a string I was holding.

'I got it!' I screamed happily and with a jerk I yanked the creature out of the water.

There it was, on the murram shore of the dam at Ol Maisor, a diminutive monster from the underworld, red and glistening, whiskers sizing up the new environment, legs already tentatively crawling their way backward towards the dam.

On the other bank, five zebra approached. They stood still a moment, looked around, and trotted, head down, to drink while their stallion watched, tail twitching at invisible flies. No breeze interrupted the dreamy heat-waves lifting from the soil, and from the thorny treetops came the joyous, powerful choir of cicadas and African birds at noon.

A dust devil swirled over madly and was soon extinguished.

'The largest crayfish I have seen in a very long time,' approved Paolo. 'Amazing how fast they grow here. I thought they only thrived in a cold climate.'

We collected a bucketful in less than two hours and drove back to Ol ari Nyiro in the evening, pursuing a herd of jumping oryx, facing a wild orange sunset, singing an Italian song, and the savannah grass was tall and streaked with mystery in the fading light.

Next day, I drove to Ngobitu's dam and ceremoniously let all the crayfish go.

'One day I'll catch you again,' I let them know. 'You and all the generations you'll produce in all the years to come.' They disappeared into the murky red water leaving just a few bubbles.

They were early days in Laikipia.

They were days of exploring, of adventure, of love and of bewilderment, when we discovered the new land we had chosen for our home, and ourselves. They were days of youth and fun, when tomorrow was still gilded, when happiness was the morning birds and the evening clouds, turquoise lizards on hot stones, weaver birds building their nests on the fever trees, dung beetles laboriously rolling huge balls, heady perfumes of wild jasmine, and the Pokot women, bare-breasted and in long skin skirts, ambling proudly along the Ol ari Nyiro boundary, head high, minding their cattle.

When I would marvel at buffalo wallowing in the mud baths, at elephant moving silently like shadows through a glade, a few metres away, unaffected by my presence. When I would stand in the night at the bottom of my new garden, almost exactly where the graves now are, a long shawl protecting me from the chill of the eastern breeze, my ears alert to hear the hyena crying on the hills and lion or leopard calling their raucous, rhythmic hunting song.

When my family was still together, and my men with me.

In the months and years which followed so much happened that I forgot my crayfish.

It was the summer of 1981, when Paolo had been a year in his grave and the tree that he had become was bearing its first flowers and the baby he had fathered, but never seen, had begun to talk, that I suddenly remembered.

'Shall we try and see if there are any crayfish in Ngobitu's dam?' I asked Emanuele. 'If they did not all die, there should be lots by now. When was it that we put them in? Five, six years ago?' We could not recall. But Emanuele, a long-limbed teenager with serious-mocking eyes, jumped on his new motorbike, carrying some defrosted meat as a bait, and disappeared in a rusty cloud of dust.

'If they are there I'll catch them. Prepare the dill and mayonnaise, Pep!'

I did not really believe we would find any. No dried-out bleached shell had been discovered along the banks –

the remnant of a stork's or heron's meal – to announce their presence. Nor, when we went out for tilapia or black bass, did we ever detect the strange shadows lurking clumsily in the shallows.

So I was immensely surprised when Emanuele appeared, triumphant, an hour or so later, carrying in his hands the largest, healthiest crayfish I had ever seen.

'There are zillions of them there,' he announced. 'We must put them on the menu.'

And so I did.

Simon my cook protested weakly, with Turkana pride, at the invasion of weird insects in his kitchen, but finally surrendered when the odd baby lobster, now attractively bright red and crowned with celery and lemon wedges, gained him additional compliments for his already outstanding cuisine.

So it was that it became a feature of hot afternoons on the ranch to go fishing, and no Venetian scampi risotto was ever tastier than the Laikipia crayfish we perfected, with lots of fresh pepper and parsley and a dash of brandy as a final touch.

But it was not just the gourmet satisfaction.

Whenever I see the crayfish at my table, I feel an immediate nostalgia, their appearance and their flavour is an instant joyous memory of other happy days, and I go back in space and season, to the time I was a little girl with pigtails and curious eyes, avidly pursuing excitement and adventure, to the unforgettable Summer of the Crayfish. The first summer I recall with my father.

*

We lived in the country, in Veneto, in a village called Crespano del Grappa, at the foot of mountain slopes covered in pine, chestnuts and *cornioli,** where my grandfather owned the silk factory. There my young father, fresh from the Second World War – where he got some medals, lost most of his friends and his dreams, but not his longing for exploring and discovering – practised medicine at the local hospital.

I was an inquisitive child, full of questions, and those early childhood days spent in the country, with any amount of space and the freedom of a large fascinating garden, a wood, an orchard, a vineyard and a stable, were to mark my life for ever. As for ever would I yearn for the outdoors, the world of imagination, of living things, of leaves and buds, of hidden nests with eggs, of sprouting seeds, of smell of grass and berries and wild shy creatures.

I was never a town girl, content to be surrounded by the noise and glitters of a modern city. On the pavements, crowded with hurrying strangers, in the lifts, speeding to vertiginous heights, in the shopping malls of marble and fountains, I felt confused and out of place. When, in the years to come, Fate brought me to travel to the world capitals, following the dream and crusade that my destiny had woven for me, I always looked for a window from where I could see the sky; for a place where to walk barefoot; for growing things alive and silent beside the man-made sophisticated junk that stifled me. All this is owed to those early days.

Inside me, bright and keen, there still is a little girl who wants to run, seak the unexplored, who loves the smell of

* A type of Italian crab-apple.

mown grass and campfires, of running water and mountain streams, of low tide and daisies in the sun and cyclamen in marvellous clumps to be discovered in the dense undergrowth.

When my mother went to have her clothes made at the house, outside the village, of a farmer's wife called Ines, who had the gift of magic hands for sewing, I often went too.

Ines worked in her kitchen. It was the largest and most comfortable room in her house, high-ceilinged, cool in the summer, when a breeze moved from the front vine pergola to the shady back garden and the vegetable patch, and cosy in the winter, when the cooking stove was crowded with pots constantly bubbling away their appetizing vapours of hearty soups and sauces.

As a result, to her annoyance, my mother's freshly delivered winter clothes all seemed to exude a smell of minestrone. Weather permitting, they had to be hung out for days before she could wear them, and sprayed with lavender and her favourite perfume, 'Fleur de Rocaille' by Caron, a festive bouquet to me exotic, inebriating, irresistible.

I was interested in this strange, different house, and observed its details with immense curiosity.

One corner of a large wooden table was covered with a grey blanket and a clean white sheet: on this Ines cut out her patterns, stencilled out of old newspapers, and stitched them with a black Singer sewing-machine.

On the mantelpiece were sepia photographs of old weddings, all the grooms identical with their heavy moustaches and ill-fitting black coats, strangled in starched collars and bow ties, ears protruding, the only variation the middle or side partings of their brilliantine-sleeked hair. They stood rigid, their hands on a papier mâché column, or on the back of an ornate chair where the brides sat. These were identical too, jowly, black-eyed, trussed up in corsets which could not disguise their florid good health, stolidly staring at the camera with incurious diffidence.

There were oval portraits of long-lost grandmothers, a faded photograph of Pio X, the *Papa Sarto*, next to vivid depictions of the sacred, bloody heart of Christ, a flame emanating from its middle; a crucifix with a shrivelled olive twig stuck behind it from last Palm Sunday; a doll dressed in pink lace, a few trinkets won at the village fair.

Ines was thin for an Italian woman of her age, with a sallow complexion from lack of sunshine. She wore an apron tucked about with needles, and her permed black hair was streaked with grey.

Chickens sometimes wandered in through the open door, with a blade of sun and dancing midges, and ventured tentatively on the white and black tiles, one foot at a time, observing me sidelong, with red-rimmed eyes.

If the session trailed on too long, I was allowed to go out to explore the sunny fields, provided I stayed within the compound. So it was that one day I ventured to the stream which formed a still pond set in a clump of mulberry trees below the house. I peered into the dark green waters and glimpsed a curious shadow like a long weird insect, hiding below a stone next to my laughing mirrored image.

It was that time of childhood when everything is new and exciting, of vivid physical impressions, smells of new places and animals, tastes of new fruit.

The scent of humid earth, of ferns and cyclamen in the recesses of the wood's undergrowth; the floury sweetness of the first roast chestnut, warm and slightly burned; the surprising variations in the odours of rabbit or goat droppings, chicken coop or geese, pigsty or stable, of horses and cows; the subtle delicious differences in the taste of roast pigeon and duck breast; of fresh raspberry or blackberry, currants or small wild strawberry; of milky new hazelnuts or walnuts, of different types of grapes. The white nuances of jasmine or wild gardenias, tuberose or lily of the valley.

It was a constant joy, living in the unpolluted country with a whole world to explore, and I shall carry with me always memories of 'first times', vivid and fresh of a thousand details.

The intoxicating sharp *corniola* wine, a forbidden sip quickly offered by a laughing maid, Lidia, a relative of Ines's, when she took us once to her parents' farmhouse on an afternoon walk, a blessed diversion which I begged her to repeat. A free new universe unfolded there for me in all its marvels, unknown to my parents. I helped to harvest, picking with my small hands, the heavy sun-warm grapes coated in verdigris, and put them in a wide basket of woven reeds; I watched mesmerized the winy juice spurt purple in the barrels through stamping toes on late September afternoons; I helped with the milking, sitting in the dark stable, pungent cow dung heavy in my nostrils; following Lidia's brothers I climbed haystacks smelling of freshly mown grass, lucerne and wildflowers and, astride a cherry tree's branch, amongst its leaves like a bird, I ate cherries until I felt like bursting; copying the other children, I kept the stones in my cheek and spat them out all at once, trying to hit my friends and laughing with abandon.

Small things were treasures, mysteries, objects of curiosity and investigation: a dead water rat in a mossy hole, with stiff whiskers and bared yellow teeth, a lizard decomposing in the sun by a clump of forget-me-not; drinking reverently from the sacred spring in a shady glade below the hill of Covolo. There – Lidia narrated – the Virgin Mary appeared to a lost, thirsty, pious child shepherdess, and stuck three of her holy burning fingers into the rock, creating three holes from which fresh clean water spurted instantly. Like a minor Lourdes, the springs of *Tre-Busi** had become a place of worship, and a monastery had been built up the hill, destination of many of our afternoon walks. We reached it along a steep, dusty white gravel road, flanked at regular intervals by *capitelli*,† filled with votive tributes of flowers and silver hearts, where the story was told in naïve oleographic frescoes.

Oh donna donna
donna lombarda
vieni stasera a ballare con me.
E io si
che vegnaria
ma ho il marito e non e non posso venir . . .‡

---

* 'Three holes' in Venetian dialect.
† Shrines.
‡ 'Oh you woman from Lombardia/come tonight and dance with me./ Oh yes oh yes, I would come with thee/but I am married and cannot go.'

We returned singing old ballads, of love stories and betrayals and honour vindicated, and passion and tears, and stopped halfway for our *merenda** of bread and cheese and raspberry syrup, sitting on the grass in the shade of a chestnut tree. There, looking down at the valley, I loved to search out my grandfather's house, disguised by a green clump of Cedars of Lebanon, next to the *filanda*† which was always easy to find, marked by its tall, smoky chimney made of old bricks.

In this bucolic contest of magical country delights, the discovery of the quaint, odd fish was intoxicating.

That evening I could not resist the temptation to recount it, and described to my father, with a wealth of details, the mysterious creature that I thought I had seen. My father listened, with the attention he always paid to my stories, and understood; and thus began the magic, exhilarating Summer of the Crayfish.

My father, with the enthusiasm and abandon that destined him to be forever young, forever inspiring, loved to find special gifts of wild morsels, gourmet foods that nature reserved for her followers, the tireless walkers, the early risers, the mountain climbers, the ones who deserved the privilege. He told us stories of handfuls of raspberries picked while running from enemy fire, of *porcini* mushrooms discovered on perilous banks inaccessible to the lazy; and the crayfish discovery coloured those mid-summer days with excitement and anticipation.

'They must be crayfish, so rare in these waters, and quite

* Snack.
† Silk factory.

delicious. We'll go fishing tomorrow night, and you will come too, because it is your discovery and you must guide me.' My father knew how to touch a deep chord of pride in my eager small heart. I was perhaps five, and not normally allowed out after dark: the exception lent my day an unbearable thrill.

We left together in the evening like conspirators, taking with us a packed dinner of sandwiches, torches and blankets and bits of meat and old salami as bait. I brought my father to the pond in the clump of trees. We peered, searching the water with the torch. My heart beat wildly: had it been an illusion? On the gravel of the bottom, amongst the stones and watercress, two grey shapes armed with claws were fighting silently.

'Well done!' approved my father, my hero, and the night glowed with my tumultuous pride.

The imprudent shellfish, attracted by the meat effluvia dissolving in the current and by the torchlight, were easily captured, and put into a tin bucket. I helped, holding the torch, carrying the bucket, and my father taught me how to grab the crayfish, just below their pincers, so they could not nip us. Splattered in mud, wet and shivering, I fell asleep exhausted in my blanket on the way back.

The crayfish were quite elusive. We could only catch a few at the time, not enough for a meal. We decided to store them at home, in one of the tanks at the back of the silk factory, a deep old cement tub where it was exciting to see the ghostly figures disappear in the mossy depths.

We went back almost every night. My father pointed out remote stars and taught me their names, we sang the partisan songs of the last war, and I was elated. The flavour of escapade, the new independence, the sounds of the night appealed to my imagination, and the experience had borders of reverie like a summer tale.

As the season progressed, the shapes became numerous in the silk factory tank.

It was finally September, the time of harvest and of returning to town, where, for the first time, I would go to school. The night of the crayfish dinner arrived.

My father surprised me by not helping with the recapture of the crayfish from their tank: this occasion was tame, and a net was produced.

He only appeared at dinner time, when already a delicious aroma was filling the house, of white wine and olive oil, and herbs and garlic.

I had been worried about eating the creatures I had come to know so well, but when they appeared on the silver platters, crowned with lemon wedges, I was startled to see my old grey friends changed to red glistening jewels. Their transformation took away my guilt. They no longer looked like those little monsters I had observed fighting in the still, silent waters and, following the others, I ate them with glee. Of the flavour, I only remember it was one of the most surprisingly delicious I had ever tasted.

No one knew that secretly, that afternoon, I had taken two couples from the full buckets and put them back furtively in the tank where they had survived so well for a month. By now, a thousand crayfish perhaps fill the tanks and ponds of that forgotten garden.

That evening, while the lamp threw weird patterns on to

the white linen table-cloth monogrammed with my grand-mother's initials, I looked at my father across the table, pensively sucking a claw, and knew that he already missed the adventure, and would have approved of my secret.

And once more, in his green, short-sighted eyes, I recognized myself.

Remember the Seagulls

For Livio

But Jonathan Livingston Seagull was not a common bird
. . . more than anything he loved to fly.

RICHARD BACH, *Jonathan Livingston Seagull, A Story*

During one of my rare visits to Italy a couple of years ago, returning from a delicious lunch of fish and chilled wine in the *valle** of a friend, I found myself driving through the piazza of Jesolo which had been so familiar to me over twenty years earlier, before I came to live in Africa and turned that page of my life for ever.

There was a grey stillness in the early April afternoon, a familiar humidity, and the smell of freshwater seaweeds from the invisible lagoon came through the car window, bringing back memories, and a sudden nostalgia.

On the spur of the moment I turned to my friend Marisa, companion of many expeditions and European peregrinations.

'Shall we go to Cavallino? I haven't been back since 1972. It's only a few miles from here.'

*A geographical characteristic of the Venetian lagoon.

She turned her red head and the gold-flecked eyes flashed the quick smile which had earned her the nickname 'Fox'.

'Why not? Are you sure you can handle it? It will be changed. Maybe no one is there.' She had been one of our frequent guests in the past.

'Let's try. It will be ages before I come this way again. Perhaps I never will.'

With instant silent agreement she steered her silver-grey Mercedes to the right, and in a few moments we crossed the small bridge, out on to the white gravel of the dirt-road on the canal dyke, and we were on our way.

The slopes were covered in fresh tall grass; a few primroses had begun to sprout, and creamy calla lilies along the banks on the water edge.

I recognized the turns of the track, the narrow, late-nineteenth-century red-brick peasant dwellings on the other side of the canal, small ploughed vegetable patches, a vine twisting into a pergola, fields of asparagus, a row of peach trees. Somehow things looked smaller and the distance was shorter than I recalled.

The road turned sharply right, the view opening out to the sea, the island of Burano in the distance, and there, suddenly, was a courtyard, a gracious brick house covered in green creepers mirrored in the still water of the lagoon, familiar outbuildings. We were there.

Our car came to a halt, skidding on the gravel. There was no other vehicle parked in the drive, and the dark green wooden shutters were closed. It looked as if there was nobody around. After a moment's hesitation, I opened the car door.

A muffled noise of voices and of boxes dragged on a cement floor came from a low construction on the right, below which there was a boathouse built straight on to the darkish water. Framed through its porch were a few white egrets in the distance, standing amongst the rushes on the *barena*,* which looked as barren and wild as ever. Two large seagulls flew over slowly, and as I followed them with my eyes, I noticed that someone was looking out of the *cavana*.†
I turned.

There was no reason why he should have known me after twenty-two years, appearing unexpectedly, out of context as I had, but I would have recognized his face anywhere.

He wore waders and an oilcloth windbreaker over a sailor's sweater as he had the last time I had seen him. The woollen cap covered half his face, and kind black eyes lit up amongst the wrinkles dug by years of squinting through autumn fogs, of peering into shallow waters for darting sea-bass spawn. His skin was burned a dark copper even though he had sheltered it with calloused hands while scanning the sky in countless summer suns, trying to spot the first duck migrating back from the north.

It took him only a moment, and all at once his arms lifted in surprise and welcome, his hand was raised to his cap, his mouth opened in the widest grin, and, without taking his eyes from my face a moment:

'*Maria, Signor, Gesù varda chi che ghe xe!*' he exclaimed in Venetian dialect. '*La signora la xe tornada. La signora*

---

* A sandbank or shoal.
† Venetian term for boathouse.

24

Kuki!* We moved forward at the same time and almost embraced. We halted, holding each other's hands.

'*Livio! Nol xe cambià. Come falo a recordarse de mi?*'† I answered automatically in an idiom I had not used in years. I was overwhelmed. Although I had hoped that I would find him, I had not really expected to do so.

Livio had been Paolo's headman in the *valle*, the head fisherman, the head hunter and the game warden. A typical product of the *valle* where he was born and whose secrets he knew, he was the invaluable collaborator on whom Paolo had relied totally. Competent, honest, of good disposition, he loved his job and excelled at it. Over the years he had become a trusted friend.

Then Paolo went to Africa and never came back. When Paolo died I received a cable: 'We send you and the children our heart-felt condolences for Dr Paolo's sad demise. Famiglia Dalla Mora.'

I had not had contact since.

With instant recognition, he greeted Marisa too; she had not changed much since the old days.

I wondered at the long memories of people who live in remote spots. It happens always in Africa: one meets someone in some god-forsaken place, and is recognized instantly, as if nothing had happened to fog the memory in the intervening time.

He insisted on giving us a *caffè corretto*,‡ and showing us

---

* 'Mary, Lord, Jesus, look who is here! Signora has come back!'
† 'Livio! You haven't changed. How can you still recognize me?'
‡ Coffee with a measure of strong liqueur added, traditional in Veneto in winter.

the house. With trepidation I entered rooms that had been familiar, climbed stairs that had felt Paolo's rapid step, Emanuele's little boy's run.

I looked out at the unchanged expanse of water from the small windows of the altered dining room, where the sound of laughter and popping corks had risen high in days gone by. Only the tall smoky chimney had not been touched.

Cavallino had been Paolo's and his first wife's place. I had never really considered it my home in the three years or so before coming to Africa, when I had often stayed there, while I was still living with my mother in the country. Yet I had felt its spell, the charm of its old stones and sleepy past, the beauty of the lagoon bathed in the mercury and coral of September sunsets, the ancient rhythm of traditions on which the life of a fishing *valle* was based. For Paolo, it had been a consolation while he waited to return to Kenya, the place to which he had discovered he belonged.

We went from room to room and sat finally, sipping our coffee in the dark dining room, where game wardens and *valle*-hands had gathered after long fishing or shooting mornings, to eat their earthy meals of crab soup and grilled eels with *polenta*, and roasted chestnuts washed down by bottles and bottles of new wine.

When we went out I noticed that a lone seagull was flying high above us and Livio followed my eyes.

'Do you remember,' he smiled at me, 'the time I gave you the seagull chicks?'

And memories flew back on still wings.

*

One afternoon, in the uncertain hour of opal before night falls, when the lagoon looks like a fluid mirror, Livio had returned from his daily tour of the locks and docked the boat inside its shelter.

Below his dark woollen beret the weather-beaten fisherman face smiled, and a hundred happy wrinkles marked his red cheeks.

'I have a present for you,' he offered in dialect. 'Come and see.'

On the bottom of the boat, beside a coil of rope on the tar-blackened planks, two brownish, fluffy birds crouched, from whose open beaks came desperate screams of hunger and terror.

'They are *magoghi*,'* said Livio proudly, 'just hatched. There were still broken shell pieces stuck to their plumes and all over the nest.'

Perhaps I did not manage to thank him. I felt bewildered and guilty that my love of animals, which was well known, had brought about this unconscious cruelty.

Through my mind darted plans to return the miserable newborn creatures to their marsh, to the beautiful destiny of which they had been for ever robbed: but the sun had set, dissolving into the water in reflections of red and mother of pearl, and there was nothing to do but agree to look after them.

It was a time when I wore long skirts in bright cotton, partly to protect my legs from the damp without wearing trousers which rubbed against the still fresh scars of my femur fracture, partly because I felt they matched the newly

* Young seagulls in Venetian dialect.

found peace, the bucolic pleasures and simplicity of country life in the Venetian *valle*.

I gathered my skirt into a nest and cautiously I lay there the birds. The gaping beaks with the pointed pink tongues, the greedy red-rimmed eyes and the ungainly cackling were far removed from the majestic grace of the adult royal seagulls they would one day become.

With little originality I remembered the story of the Ugly Duckling which like many fairytales is pervaded by the revenge of the small and humble against the wealthy and handsome. Cinderella, Snow White and armies of Thumbelinas had their animal equivalent in the ugly cygnet vindicated by Hans Christian Andersen. So, feeling like a fairy godmother, I set about caring for my wards.

To begin with I looked for an appropriate container. An old dolls' pram in green plastic looked perfect, and I lined it with wood shavings, small pieces of materials and clean rags.

Emanuele captured small fry from along the shore and presented them to me.

While I prepared their crib I kept the baby seagulls tucked into my skirt, working with one hand without noticing that the chirps had grown weak in the warm darkness of the folds. When I tried to put them in the pram they were asleep. I contemplated them for a while, still in my skirt, soft tiny balls of feathers like a Victorian muffler, one with its head below the other's wing.

When hunger woke them up hours later I was numb with stiffness.

I quietened their shrieks of outrage, forcing the fish that Emanuele handed to me down their wide throats. They devoured it voraciously, with ease born of instinct, pecking my fingers in their greed. That was probably their first meal, and it was thrilling that they accepted me so quickly. When there was no more fish, I covered the pram with a rag, and in the darkness they slept again.

That night I read what I could find about aquatic birds in Paolo's extensive library. So I came to learn of a curious experiment, performed on baby ducklings.

When the eggs were about to hatch, a few were removed from the nest and put into an incubator, a surrogate nest, where, instead of the mother duck, there was a rectangular cardboard box, tied with a string so that it could be pulled along.

The moment they broke out of their shell, the ducklings went immediately to the cardboard shape, nestling under it and moving with it whenever the string jerked it away.

At that stage they returned the ducklings to their real nest, where in the meantime the others had hatched, and were gathered around the mother duck, following her every movement. The experiment-ducklings did not join them. They remained confused, cowering in a corner until the box was placed near them, and they rushed to it with jubilant chirps. Thus was the theory confirmed that birds recognize and are imprinted by the first moving object they see after hatching from their egg.

When I put them on the bank and retreated a few paces to look at them, they rushed towards me with piercing screams, relaxing only when they managed to huddle under my skirt.

I experimented several times, my heart in my mouth, and the result was always the same. They did not follow anyone else, on the contrary they shrank from people, but at my appearance their cries changed as if they definitely recognized me. I realized that something similar to the experiment I had read about had happened to the wretched young seagulls; they had chosen me as their mother substitute.

The revelation that two royal seagull chicks, among the noblest of birds, unsurpassed masters of sea and ocean, dancers of the sky, had chosen me as their mother, humbled me, made me proud and scared me with the responsibility. In my role as mother-seagull I felt awkward and inadequate.

I decided that I must try, at least partially, to fulfil my task by teaching them to swim.

It was May. Already the days were getting longer and the sun warmed the chill water of the *colauro** where captive sea bass fattened, waiting for autumn, and eels the colour of mud slid in the weedy bottom with disquieting movements.

Next day I gently set the seagulls on the grassy slope of the canal, where seaweed and bleached crab legs dried in the sun. I moved with tentative steps into the oily cool water, feeling the mud squirm beneath my toes when they disturbed a flatfish or an eel.

The gulls came to the water edge they did not yet know, and there they stood, uncertain, stumping in the mud with spread claws, crying.

I moved deeper into the water, imitating their sounds like a farmer's wife when she calls her chickens, a comical scene to the uninitiated. But the only spectator was Emanuele, connoisseur and lover of animals and loyal supporter, who

---

* Venetian dialect: part of the canal that links the *valle* to the lagoon.

was following events from the shore, biting his finger with concentration. He was no more than four years old, and it must have been an extraordinary adventure.

Step by cautious step, shrieking unceasingly, the seagulls followed. Then they launched themselves, leaving behind them a touchingly tiny wake, like frail paper boats obliquely drifting in the current. They swam towards me with increasing confidence. From the shore Emanuele laughed and clapped.

Finally soothed, in their element, with an instinctive fluid elegance which their former awkward steps had not foreshadowed, the *magoghi* floated around my head, their tiny eyes for the first time at the same level as mine.

Every day after that first attempt, we swam together and I fed them the small fish that Emanuele managed to capture for them. Ten days or so went by.

The time of the unavoidable first separation found me nervous and uncertain, like a real mother about to leave her own newborn behind in the care of strangers. A certain premonition made me fear that something would happen to them in my absence.

It was the dog which in the night after I left broke into the bathroom where, after having fed them more than usual, I had confined them to keep them safe and comfortable.

It was a pain that I had never experienced before, a sense of failure, as if I had betrayed them, failing the universal rule of caring for the young.

It was a lesson reinforced when later I went to live in Africa, never to encourage the gift of a wild creature, which captivity would kill or make into a slave, a worse fate still.

And I saw a new meaning in the large seagull which followed our attempt at swimming, soaring and gliding in large circles over our heads, calling raucously in vain.

I looked at Livio. The afternoon was drawing on, it was getting late. The grey fog of every evening, with its drifting ghosts, was rising from the water. Time to return.

'The seagulls. Yes, of course. It was sad when they were killed, but perhaps it was as well. As much as I loved them, I could never have taught them how to fly.'

We embraced with promises of writing, keeping in touch. I knew I might never return.

We drove off. I looked back before turning. The house was fading in the mist, silent, with all its past untold and unrevealed.

Livio's figure was silhouetted against the sky, a hand still raised in farewell.

The seagull had disappeared.

A Dance of Spiders

It was as though, in that remote corner of the world, I
had received a sinister hint as to the existence of certain
influences outside the palpable terrestrial sequences of life.

LLEWELYN POWYS, *Black Laughter*

'A tragic thing has happened. I am terribly sorry.' The voice
was serious, strangely hesitant. I tightened my grip on the
telephone receiver.

A silence, charged with premonition of doom.

'It's Julius.'

The red-haired man swallowed another sip, and his restless,
intelligent eyes became misty behind his thick glasses. I was
glad I had fixed him a very strong whisky: it looked as if he
would need every drop.

In the candlelight of the sitting room of my Nairobi house,
his face was lustrous with sweat. His eyelids were red-rimmed,
and there was a slight tremor in the hand which held the
glass. His voice had an inspired intonation, the emphatic
quality of Sunday sermons, the sternness of Dickensian
teachers in young boys' schools.

'Talk,' I encouraged him. 'I think it would help you if you could tell me the story from the beginning. How did you meet Julius?'

His freckled face lit up in a smile.

'I will never forget the first time I saw him. Many years ago, when I had just begun teaching at Amani Boys School, I went with a colleague to a Kikuyu village looking for candidates for a scholarship to the school. He stood out amongst all those boys with a presence that struck me instantly. The peasants listening to him hung silently on his lips. Still so small, he was aloof, unreachable. From that moment I loved him.'

A glazed look clouded his eyes.

'He was nine years old.'

The early afternoon sun brightened the fields of coffee bushes and the red wet earth trampled by many feet. Banana trees, planted in clumps, shaded rows of young maize shoots. A mottled group of cattle, goats and a few hispid, mud-spattered sheep grazed off the long elephant grass that grew green and abundant on the slopes of Kiambu. Grey clouds, just emerging from the horizon, announced the daily evening storm of the short rains. From the country church, a melodious sound flew in waves, young voices singing a lilting hymn that came from distant lands.

Standing in the churchyard, facing an audience of villagers of all ages and both sexes, was the church choir of young boys. They wore long robes of vivid blue, with wide white collars falling over their shoulders. Their eyes in the dark faces were bright, imbued with a strange sense of wonder, and they sang with the rhythm and enthusiasm of innocence and unquestioning faith. Their features were still childish, unformed, smooth, the voices pure and high.

He stood out amongst them. He was not the tallest, and his harmonious voice was not the strongest.

Perhaps it was his beauty. The clear brow, the curling, girlish eyelashes, his smile. It was, perhaps, the way he held himself, radiating pride and confidence.

Perhaps it was the feeling that he was remote and difficult to conquer.

When the singing stopped the boy came forward a few steps, and walked out on to the patch of grass before mounting into the wooden pulpit. His voice was frail and crystalline, yet enhanced by a quaintly powerful authority. He addressed the colourful crowd with his religious exhortations and a spontaneous grace which went beyond prayer.

Anthony looked around, observing his fellow spectators. Old women, their grey heads in scarves, dressed in long skirts and sweaters hand-knitted in bright yarns; young women, carrying invisible sleeping infants well wrapped in pink and green lacy shawls tied to their backs; old men, young men, heads bare, still mostly in their shapeless working clothes. The lazy afternoon insects buzzed in the sun. No one moved. The crowd was spellbound, enraptured by the boy's charm. Standing in the half shade of an avocado tree, Anthony watched to the end. Then he approached.

'Would you like to study in a big school in Nairobi, where there is a great choir, and music matters?'

The boy looked up: large, liquid eyes with impossibly long, silky eyelashes. The boy smiled, a dazzling flash of even teeth like matching macadamia nuts, a warmth of honeycomb in the hazel eyes, which seemed to touch and melt something in Anthony's chest, and his legs were reduced to wax.

'Yes, I would.'

'Do you think your father will let you?'

'I have no father. He died two years ago.' A shadow drifted across his brow like a curtain which was soon lifted again. 'He drank. I have four brothers. I am the eldest.'

Anthony swallowed.

'And your mother?'

The little boy shrugged.

'She would not mind. She has much to do. There is no money and she works in the *shamba*. She also helps in the church.' His face hardened and his eyes clouded over. 'After church, she goes to the *muganga*.'

'I could look after you. I teach there. Would you like that?'

'Perhaps,' said the boy with an adult smile, 'you will let me read your books? I like to learn about animals and nature. I have no books of my own.'

Again the sudden white of even teeth.

'My name is Julius.'

'My name is Julius.'

The handsome face smiled at me and I noticed the eyes which seemed to take over most of his face.

'A good-looking young man,' I thought. He wore a pair of clean new jeans, a striped blue and white cotton shirt. A plastic watch, new and brightly coloured, was fastened round his slim wrist. I looked at his feet: good leather moccasins,

a blue pullover slung around his shoulders. His skin was an
amber brown, unblemished. Short curly hair and fine hands
with clean short nails. On his upper lip a shadow of a
moustache. He was slim, with narrow hips. Slightly effemi-
nate? There was a distinctive radiance about him which could
not be missed.

'It is very kind of you to ask me to dinner,' he said
carefully in good English. He looked up at my tall *makuti*
roof, around at the polished furniture, the gleaming copper
and brass vases. As on every night, a candle trembled in
front of the silver frame with Emanuele's photograph. A fine
blue smoke drifted from the incense holder. My eight dogs
slept on the carpets in various poses of abandoned content-
ment. Two servants in starched white uniforms were prepar-
ing the table, laying red hibiscus flowers. The fire crackled
vivaciously in the vast fireplace.

There was a candid wonder in his eyes.

'I have never been in a place like this before.'

A few weeks earlier I had received a letter, signed by
Anthony S., his teacher, sponsor and protector, who asked
if we could host in our research camp one of his most brilliant
students, the head prefect of Amani, who needed first-hand
experience in the outdoor environment in order to write a
descriptive essay which would allow him to run for a scholarship to Cambridge university.

Amani was well known for its high standards of education
and for making available superior academic training to students of underprivileged background but with good minds;
it was known to instil discipline and a sense of responsibility.
In the firmament of Kenyan schools, Amani was a shining

star, unique. There were well over a thousand students there. Whoever managed to become head prefect must have been rather unusually gifted with leadership and intelligence. But even so, Cambridge university was still as far from Amani as a distant planet.

I had been intrigued and had immediately agreed to host this boy for a month or so.

Looking at him now, I felt that I wanted to help his ambition to materialize, and that I would see more and more of him over the years. There was something special about him, which I could detect immediately, but not describe.

'I understand that you would like to read geography at Cambridge. A really ambitious plan.'

Not for a moment was there hesitation in his tone:

'I have been fortunate. I want to give back to my country what I have received over the years. Cambridge. I am sure I will enjoy it there.'

I opened my bar cabinet.

'Would you like a glass of wine?'

For a moment only, he looked lost, then he grinned.

'I would rather have a Coke, if it is all right with you. I am not used to wine.'

'We can't find Julius.'

Anthony's voice sounded tight and strangled on the phone. 'He has disappeared. Gone. I can't locate him anywhere. He is meant to leave for Cambridge in two days time. I was hoping you might have heard from him.'

His emphatic preacher's tone became a whine.

'What are we going to do?'

I answered with the calm that always prevails in me when others around me lose theirs.

'Take it easy. He is practically a man, remember? Why should he always report where he goes? He has to be able to cope on his own in England. I am sure there is a perfectly ordinary explanation. Do you have any reason to think otherwise? Perhaps he has gone to say his farewells to some friends.'

'That is exactly what I fear,' Anthony whispered.

The noise of a car engine was followed by the slamming of a door, then of another. Footsteps descended the stairs to my front door. Someone knocked. I went to open.

Julius stood forlorn on my doorstep, in a dejected attitude, head bent and the collar of his wind jacket open on his thin neck. The change from the secure, radiant boy who looked me always straight in the eyes struck me like a blow.

'Julius. Are you all right?' No answer.

'Julius, for God's sake. Come on. Come in. Tell me what's happened. It can't be as bad as that.'

A movement behind Julius, the leaves of the gardenia bush swayed. From the shadows, another shape emerged. The suddenness of the movement startled me. I caught my breath.

'Get in,' said Anthony, as if talking to a rebellious little boy who had thrown a tantrum. I noticed his eyes were enlarged. He pushed him in.

'You must confess to Kuki what has happened.'

Julius sat on my white sofa in the soft light like a culprit ready to confess a crime. The absurdity of the situation annoyed me.

'What is it?' I probed gently. 'There is nothing at all that you "have" to tell me. Your life is your life. You look fine to me. Can I help you in any way?'

'Tell her,' urged Anthony.

I braced myself for the worst, and yet I felt there was really nothing the boy could have done so tragic as to justify such attitude.

'A few years ago I met a girl,' murmured Julius in a small, dull voice. 'She was one from my native village. I have known her all my life.'

'And so?' A lightness overcame me, as if the precipice on which I was perching had revealed itself much shallower, less forbidding than I had feared.

'You must tell her. Confess what you have done.' Anthony's tone sounded absurdly serious.

'I have a son. He is three years old.'

An immense relief swept over me.

'Is that all?'

Julius looked up, and his moist eyes held an appeal. But through this, to my dismay, I read an overwhelming terror, as of a haunted animal running blindly off in the night.

'I have received this.'

He offered a crumpled sheet of paper, which blossomed in his open palm slowly, unfolding like a crushed moon flower. Words crawled over it, scribbled in pencil in gangly, uneven letters, oddly repulsive, like a dance of spiders.

'I can't read Kikuyu.'

'It is a threat.' His voice broke in a sob. 'They have put a spell on me. They do not want me to leave. If I go, I will die.'

A chill drifted through my western room, ugly with

sneering masks and unmentionable rituals, slaughtered black goats, smeared entrails on muddied feathers, beating night drums, guttural songs and young boys' fears. For only a moment its power hit me, the unease prevailed. For that moment I could believe anything, I accepted that anything could happen. Once again I knew that this world I had chosen was not just red sunsets, migrating herds, sunny savannah and bougainvillaea in bloom: I remembered the snake, the screeching of imagined brakes, the open graves, the pain, the ephemeral reality which often eluded our comprehension and mocked our bewilderment: and I realized that this, also, was Africa.

I came back to the present.

'Julius, this is 1985. You are about to go to one of the most sophisticated universities in the world. You are going to fly there in a large airplane, meet many people from all over the world, learn useful things which will, when you come back to Kenya, allow you a career that is all you have ever dreamed of. By going you are hurting no one. This is what the new Kenya is all about. They should be proud of you, back in your village.'

A thought raced quickly through my mind and I chased it off.

'Who is it? Who has written this? Who has put a spell on you?'

His face had closed like a slab of stone, and I could see I would not learn it from him. Not now. Even as I was asking I knew that he would not tell.

'They think that I will not come back. They think I will be out of their influence.'

'The girl's family? Do you care for this girl?'

Julius had no time to answer.

Anthony looked up sharply with pressed lips.

'He does not see that girl any more. It was just a mistake. It was her fault. The girl has given up any hope about him. An ignorant peasant girl. She was compensated.' He waved the shadow of the girl aside like an insignificant moth.

I reacted.

'However, her family may think otherwise.'

Julius looked up at me with a sudden resolution in his eyes. I read confusion, fear, hatred and resignation all at once in the look he gave me. I read something else also, deep and murky, unspeakable and terrifying, which I could not interpret.

I cleared my throat.

'You must go ahead and nothing is going to happen to you. Nobody can hate you just because you go to school to learn. Spells and *muganga* cannot hurt you if you do not believe in them.'

With immense horror, I realized he did.

A shiver of rain forest and dark huts, green smoke and voodoo passed again over the glittering crystal table. As in a Gothic tale, in my imagination the candles flickered uncertainly.

The sound was low and hoarse, it was his voice no longer. It rustled like a snake and I recoiled.

'The girl did not go to the *muganga*. It was my mother.'

Three years later.

I closed the heavy door, the chill of November behind

me. The bright light caught me unprepared, blinding me for a moment. The vast room was full of people and the noise of conversation echoed from the high vaulted ceiling.

I focused on the unreal scene with wonder.

The elephants moved in their cages set in a circle, swaying their sad grey heads rhythmically from left to right and from right to left.

Waiters in white jackets and white gloves circulated through the guests offering trays of canapés and cocktails. The air was warm, humid; candles glowed trembling in silver chandeliers. I looked around recognizing some familiar faces, and then I saw him.

Holding his glass of wine, still intact, dressed in a blue suit and starched shirt, a very good silk tie impeccably knotted, Julius smiled his disarming warm smile at me across the room.

An elephant trumpeted, interrupting all chatter of conversation for a few moments. The whiff of steaming dung could not be disguised by the mixture of perfumes and cigarette smoke. It was a very weird setting for a cocktail party, the Elephant House at London Zoo.

Julius had been asked as my guest.

'Thank you for inviting me. I feel somewhat overwhelmed.'

So did I for that matter. The absurdity of the occasion stood between us like a pond to cross, and I smiled.

'These poor creatures. And all the real ones, the free ones that we have left back home.'

He scowled, the corners of his mouth turned down,

betraying an undisguised nostalgia. For an instant the sadness of the exiled elephant was his same sadness.

'Anthony tells me that you took to Cambridge like a duck to water.'

He looked groomed and confident enough, very much in command in what truly was an unusual environment.

Despite – or possibly because of – the trapped miserable elephant, it was a long step from Africa.

He grimaced, waving his full glass gingerly. 'I like it there; but I still cannot drink the wine.'

I noticed that his fingers held the stem very tightly, with white knuckles. For a moment I thought he was going to snap it. A black crocodile-skin strap circled his thin wrist setting off a new gold watch.

'Are you sure you are all right, Julius? Are you looked after? Are you very homesick?'

Such a long step, I thought, from those mud huts, the thatched grass roofs, the banana clumps and the smiling girls with high breasts and singing eyes. Such a long step from his real roots. If I felt somehow out of place, how would he feel? Social superficial chatter, witty whimsical remarks, politics, the economy, the last show, what happened to those rhino in Meru, the price of ivory, absurd about rhino horn trade, is Leakey's appointment really going to make a difference to Kenya's wildlife?

A lady in a black velvet suit, a blonde lock falling artily over one eye, took hold of Julius's elbow, swept him away effortlessly and in seconds he was lost in the crowd.

For a moment I saw him as a shipwrecked sailor taken away by the tide, never to be reached; I felt I had to rescue him; then someone attracted our attention by chiming on a crystal glass, and the speeches began. When I looked again for him, he was gone.

'Julius, Julius, how nice to have you back!'

He had grown a light moustache.

'I passed the exams at Cambridge. Now I think I will go for a Ph.D.'

He seemed thinner, taller. His accent was more polished, the words chosen slowly and with care. He was detached even when answering. I felt his laughter as a superficial way of hiding a deeper concern. There were corners of his personality where he did not allow anyone to probe; what did he have to hide? What was he afraid of? What tangled cobwebs hid behind the sunny boy's mask?

'Anthony came to fetch me at the airport.'

'Nice of him, at that hour. How is Anthony?'

He lifted his shoulder with a distant look.

'I had not seen him in months. I have a girlfriend.'

He looked me straight in the eye.

'He does not approve.'

And added, in a hiss that startled me by its concentrated spite:

'As if I cared.'

'A girlfriend, but that is great, Julius! Who is she?'

'Her name is Olinda. We live together now. I love her very much.'

To my surprise, his eyes filled suddenly with tears:

'She is so beautiful.' He whispered it with a longing in his voice, as if talking of a fairy which eluded him.

'You must be happy, we must celebrate. It is your life. You are in your twenties. It is perfectly normal for you to fall in love. I think it is wonderful. Anthony must accept this, of course.'

What had never been said struck me, and the time was right to finally bring it into the open.

'He loves you too,' I added gently.

'I know. But that is not the problem. I can deal with Anthony.' A far-away look. 'I have done it all my life.'

'Why are you so sad then? What is there to disturb you? Perhaps you can tell me? Perhaps I can be of some help?'

Tears were rolling down his cheeks uncontrollably. I took his hand in mine and guided him unresisting to my office.

'She is of the Luo tribe.'

The phrase fell like a stone in a still pond and even I was overwhelmed by its ripples.

A Luo girl and a Kikuyu boy!

The Luo tribe is spread around the warm shores of the great Lake Victoria, in western Kenya; the Kikuyu, as one knows, originate from the cold forest areas all around Mount Kenya's snowy slopes. Worlds apart, they have always been traditional enemies. Their people are physically and ethnically different. Language, appearance, customs, taste, habits, beliefs are totally opposite, deep-rooted. Even in this modern Kenya this was a very difficult – practically an impossible – match. Its implications dumbfounded me for a moment. I brushed them off.

'It does not matter, surely? She lives here in the town, far from the lake. Her people, you say, are reasonably comfortable. She is educated. She is emancipated. What does her tribe matter if she loves you too?'

'It is my mother. She will never agree. She has told me that she will curse me for ever if I marry her. I want to marry her,' he added with a sob.

I looked at him, bewildered.

'If I do not have my mother's blessing as tradition asks, our children will be cursed for ever.'

He looked at me through his tears.

The words rose from the Middle Ages, in one stroke wiping out years of education, Cambridge, books, culture, gold watch, computers, driving licence:

'She is uncircumcised.'

And so it came out, in my tame Nairobi office filled with photographs and books, the pine panelled walls that smell of the forests on the Great Rift where the wood came from. The place high on the Kinangop where Julius' mother lives, still now.

With her memories, and perhaps with her remorse.

He found her one day, that woman who was his mother, that peasant girl who had grown old too quickly through her labour, creeping about in the Nairobi flat that he shared with Olinda.

She shrank at his sight, hissing like a lizard, her headscarf half undone, trying to hide something in her apron.

He forced open her clamped hand, and recoiled in horror.

It looked like a small, dead animal, hairy and still. A thick, repulsive tangle of curly human hair, fashioned as a doll. Two rusty pins stuck out of its tiny head, like grotesque horns.

'How did you get Olinda's hair? How did you find us? How could you come in? You have never been here before.'

He pushed her away in fury, confused, afraid, angry, yet hopelessly dependent on his mother's fierce attachment, her resilient strength, her earthy power and the magnetic eyes which had subjugated him since his childhood.

I listened without ever interrupting him. He looked up through the veil of tears.

'The problem is that I love my mother. Love is not a feeling that she understands. She was married at puberty, soon after her circumcision, in exchange for a few goats and some gourds of beer, to a much older man she did not even know. He drank. He used her and beat her up every night. All day she worked the *shamba* cutting the red soil with her *jembe* to plant beans, potatoes and maize, with me and then my brothers and sisters tied to her bent back.'

He went on.

'When the coffee was ripe after the season of the rains, she went to pick it at sunrise with the other women. They were each given a large metal *debe* and they had to fill it with the red berries. They sang while they worked and those songs were my earliest music. She was quick and still so young, so supple, almost a child, she could fill even ten *debes* sometimes. They were paid a few coins each time. In those days the coins were made of brass and glinted like gold in the sun; many still had a hole in the middle below the portrait of King George, so the people could put a leather string through them, and hang them round their neck. No one had purses, nor pockets in those times.

'In the afternoon she chopped firewood from the forest and

tied it in immense bundles, which she carried on her back: she had to strap the new baby to her chest instead, so it could nurse. She smelled of milk and sweat and wood smoke, and we felt secure in her warmth. The load was held by a leather strip tied around her forehead, and it was so heavy that it left a permanent ridge-mark over her brows. Loaded like a donkey she staggered home after dusk to cook our meal.

'We lived, cooked, ate, slept in one smoky room without a chimney. The fire's smoke choked us and gave us red eyes and sore throats; we all caught pneumonia sooner or later as the breath of the night outside was chilly, when we had to go out and relieve ourselves in the pit latrine in the bamboo thicket. She gave us a brew of honey and some bitter herbs and we were cured. But it was cosy, safe and warm inside our mud hut, like a den in the forest. There were scorpions and centipedes in the roof, sometimes black house-snakes, but it was too smoky for mosquitoes and too cold for malaria and too dark for flies. It was fine. There were only two makeshift beds. We children all shared a mattress filled with straw on a low pallet made of rough branches.'

I listened without interrupting him, fascinated.

'My father drank *changaa* until he recognized nobody. The whites of his eyes became yellow and stared unseeing. I tried not to hear their noises in the dark. But it was never really dark with those red fizzing embers. Once, when he beat her up more wildly I stood up to him. I was six years old. He knocked me off towards the wall, blinded by fury. For a few days I could not move, all my body ached. Soon after this, my father left us to marry a younger girl.'

He went on.

49

'My mother never accepted his second wife. There were terrible scenes and she screamed; she never cried. Tears were not something traditional for the Kikuyu girls in the old days. She was intelligent, although she could neither read nor write. As a child she had learned to sing hymns at the Mission church, she had a clear high voice and could remember sounds. She never knew what she was singing though, apart from the Kikuyu hymns. She never learned any English. I went with her. That's how I learned to sing.

'She cleaned the church for a few shillings a week. She began to spend much of that money and the coffee cents with the village *muganga*. She did spells against the other wife. She could not see the contradiction between the Christian god she served and the pagan spirits she summoned to her help.

'The *muganga* was a very old man covered in monkey skins, with long hair in matted locks. He wore bizarre ornaments of teeth, dried hoofs and bones, and he stank of coagulated blood and strange herbs. Purses hung from a leather belt, he wore sandals made of raw hides, he scowled at us with red wild eyes, and I was afraid of him. He lived alone on a hill out of the village with a few black goats, next to a large *mugumu* tree. All children were terrified of him and we ran away when he approached.

'To perform her sorceries, my mother had to procure certain items that he ordered her to find from time to time. To perpetrate a really powerful incantation a goat was always slaughtered, her bowels examined and scattered with strange rituals, potions of roots and powders boiled up and, some-times, for a sickness or a death spell, weird dolls made to

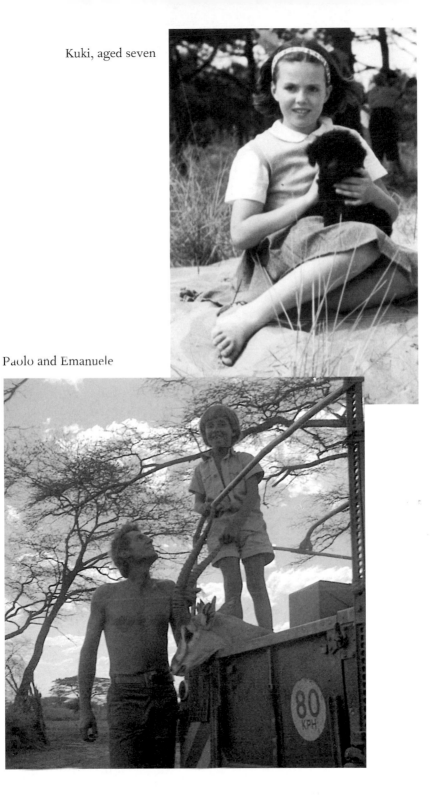

Kuki, aged seven

Paolo and Emanuele

Emanuele and Kuki

Kuki and her pack of Alsatians at Kuti

Buffalo at Chui Dam, Ol ari Nyiro

The fire at Abukari barely missed our plane and our tent

The mangrove forest at low tide, Abukari

Aidan landing at Abukari

Sveva fishing at Abukari

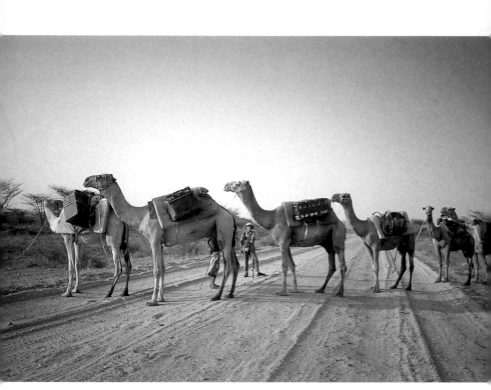

Above The road to Isiolo

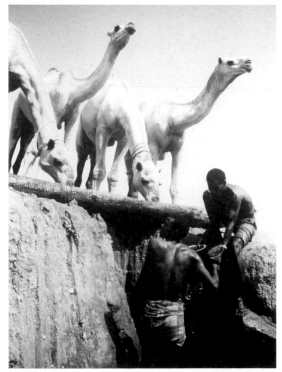

Left The wells at Koiya with Ahmed Nyeusi and Ahmed Nyukundu

The team of the camel expedition at Il baa Okut

Lolokwe, the last night. Farewell to Racub

Mote and Sveva at Abukari

resemble the person who had to suffer. You know, people died of spells very easily. Or sometimes they went mad. They still do. Those dolls had to contain a bit of hair of the victim, or perhaps some fragment of his fingernails, a piece of material from his clothes. The puppet had to be placed secretly somewhere in the victim's house or on her or his person; a pin had to go through the part of the body where the disease was meant to appear.

'Occasionally one saw someone moving around in a trance, as if sleepwalking, with a vacant stare, and we knew that a spell had been put on them. If the *muganga* who was responsible was not found and compelled to give an antidote to neutralize the witchcraft, the person lost all interest in life, stopped eating, and went off like a candle.

'My father died a few years after. They found his mangled body in a ditch one morning. The hyena had found him first. They said he had fallen in drunk. Perhaps this was true. But he had been seen looking wild and going around in circles, and I wondered.'

'Your mother would not do that to your girlfriend. Surely not. That's evil, Julius!'

He looked up at me without answering.

Then he murmured something in a half voice, something quite unbelievable, which I was not sure I had heard correctly.

He asked me then if he could be in Laikipia for two weeks, staying in the empty house overlooking the forest at Enghelesha, far from the crowds and problems, unreachable even by his girlfriend.

He had to think, rest his soul, reflect, be alone.

I saw him a few times. He was aloof, remote more than ever, closed in a world of his own. He had lost much weight. As if he no longer cared for his appearance, he had begun to grow a beard.

I invited him for a picnic at a dam one Sunday, and he came. He did not eat. He sat on a rock at a distance, throwing pebbles in the water absently, only occasionally taking part in the conversation.

'What are you doing all day?'

'I read.'

'What do you read?'

'I read Shakespeare.' And with a shadow of his old humour he added: 'It is so grand reading Shakespeare aloud looking down at the Rift Valley at sunset.'

I could not agree more.

Shakespeare, Cambridge, the *muganga*, the rural super-stition, the deeply rooted beliefs, his English tutor's influence, his studies, his Luo girlfriend from the great lake, this new overwhelming love and passion that he was so unprepared to handle, his terrible mother.

I was seriously worried for Julius.

I never saw him again. It was three months after that Sunday when my phone had rung with the tragic news.

'It's Julius. He has committed suicide.'

Sitting now on my white sofa, gulping down whisky absently like one who never drinks strong alcohol and could not care less about the consequences, Anthony went on talking.

'I had seen him a few days before. I found him in his room. He sat on his bed and looked at me with empty eyes,

drawn, not listening. He had grown an untidy, long beard.
He looked like someone under a witchcraft spell.'

I bolted.

'He had a book of Shakespeare next to him. He was
reading *Romeo and Juliet*.'

A pair of star-crossed lovers.

A pause.

'He swallowed rat poison. His mother was furious when
he died.'

'Furious? Not sad? Not desperate?'

'Angry, as if something had gone wrong.'

Wrong?

What was it that Julius had said to me that day long ago,
in my office? It was important that I should remember.
Something about the spell. The hair. Olinda's hair. No. Not
Olinda's. The spell was not for her. It was for Julius. So that
he would lose interest in her, leave her. The spell went
wrong. Everything now was clear.

He had lost, instead, all interest in life.

His voice came back from distances to whisper:

'It was MY hair in the doll.'

Why an Elephant?

O my America! my new-found-land.

JOHN DONNE, *Elegies, On Going to Bed*

I

'*Dear Mrs Gallmann*' – the letter said – '*Thank you for allowing us to stay in the Education Centre in memory of your late son. I wish I had met him. I loved everything, but mostly the wildlife. The first animal I saw was an elephant. I had never seen one before. It was very big, I could see him from far.*
    Anne Wanjoi, Nyahururu Secondary School, Ngarua'

On the large rock set in the middle of the yard, a red hibiscus beckons in the breeze.

'*Felix qui potuit rerum cognoscere causas*'*

says the inscription from Virgil, on the brass plaque. And, underneath:

* 'Happy he who can understand the causes of things' – Virgil.

In Memory of Emanuele.

Venezia 1966 – Laikipia 1983.

Two acacia trees, one small, one large, the symbol of survival and of hope, are engraved below.

A short life, an entire story in a few words.

I am at the Laikipia Wilderness Education Centre, built of stones and thatch in the heart of the ranch where I live and where my son died and was buried at seventeen, one sunny day of April in 1983.

Yet, in the agony of his loss, slowly, like the secret buried seed which finds the strength to sprout, forcing its way up towards light and life, I found the key to survival. I understood that Emanuele, like Paolo before him and all the ones who had gone ahead faster than us, had simply changed dimension, and that, if I could no longer see his body, I could always feel the power of his essence, of which I was myself part. There were no boundaries.

I founded the mission to work positively for as long as I could, to justify my existence and my survival by using my opportunities to make a change.

I soon discovered that there was no end to the possibilities brought about by this new energy. Emanuele had gone to join Paolo, but the power of his love and memory, reflected in the African nature that he had loved, became my inspiration to create something long-lasting, that time could not tarnish.

Walking alone on the hills and in the valleys of this place he had loved above all, I decided to open its door to other young people like him: enthusiastic, fond of the wild, with a sense of purpose, so that they might learn to understand, and so to respect, Africa.

Only two generations ago Africans knew all there was to know about their environment. They lived in harmony with their surroundings, which in turn provided them with food and medicine. They survived by hunting and fishing, collecting plants and tubers, gathering honey and wild berries, without destroying the subtle, fragile balance of their ecosystem on which their very existence depended. In those days they were familiar with their roots, they had pride in their customs and traditions, they valued their world, and they knew elephants. Those days are no longer.

Unless the new generation, now converging on urban areas to be educated in alien skills imported from a far-away world, is given the chance to experience the wilderness which was their immediate ancestors' familiar domain, to be proud of their land and its unrepeatable beauty, there will be no hope for the ecology of this continent. The forests will go, and the plants and the biodiversity and then the birds and the animals, and Africa will remain a mangled landscape, ravaged by droughts and floods.

I believe that childhood impressions live in us to guide our adult behaviour. This is the principle that guided me when I created the Wilderness Centre.

On a day like any other, sitting on the look-out built at the end of the promontory on which the school stands, on the shores of a small dam covered with clumps of papyrus and frequented by water birds, I watch a herd of impala coming gracefully down to the water to drink. Egyptian geese fly off, screaming, in a flutter of wings. Behind them, a water buck, and from the *lelechwa* shrubs, one after the other, file the elephants.

Standing on the shore, in their colourful school uniforms, a group of African children watch in awe.

2

The young man in the neat, well-cut blue suit held a card with my name, misspelled.

'It's me you are looking for.' I introduced myself, and he flashed back a frank open smile which split his pleasant dark face in a happy grin.

'I was not quite sure of the spelling. I hope you had a good flight.'

I was tired, coming in from a few days of work and promotion in Seattle, still jet-lagged, but looking forward to exploring this part of California. The air was warm but surprisingly dry. The sun shone. From the sky Los Angeles's suburbia had looked like an arid, overcrowded third world city of endless, low, identical buildings.

I followed him through the crowd.

'Let's take my luggage and then we go.'

He took my computer case and glanced quickly at me.

'I cannot place your accent.' He was self-assured. 'Where are you from?'

I laughed.

'I am originally Italian. I thought everyone could detect my accent as soon as I open my mouth.' My Italian accent has not faded after more than twenty years in Africa. I am rather proud of it, and in any case there is not much I can do to improve it.

After all, I was once Italian.

'Oh I love Italy. I flew here with Alitalia and they said "*Signore e Signori, benvenuti a bordo*".' We laughed together. 'It sounded so nice I would have liked them to repeat it again and again. Where do you live in Italy?'

'Well, I actually no longer live there. I live in Africa.'

He stopped abruptly.

'Where, in Africa?'

For the first time I noted that his accent was not American; I had taken for granted from the beginning he was an African American. Now I looked at him better.

Slim, of medium height, intelligent eyes, small ears, regular, slightly familiar features.

'I live in Kenya.'

Even before I said it I anticipated what was going to happen, but still his joy took me by surprise.

'*Oh jambo! jambo jambo mama. Hata mimi natoka Kenya. Mimi ni Jaluo. Halla bahati mʒuri sana kukutana na wewe hapa.*' I come from Kenya too. I am a Luo tribesman. What strange good luck to meet you here.

How lucky indeed. That the person sent to meet me in Los Angeles where I went because of the planned feature film based on my autobiography, *I Dreamed of Africa*, is an African and a Kenyan, and this by pure coincidence, cannot be a coincidence. It is an omen. A fantastically good omen.

That set the mood.

I am delighted; a chance to speak Swahili during this trip.

We find the luggage, he goes and gets the car. A comfortable, dark blue, normal-looking limousine, not, thank goodness, one of those over-long vulgar affairs.

We settled in and I asked him about his life. How and why did he get here?

He drove with easy assurance.

'I had a dream,' he said, 'of becoming a business administrator. I wanted to go to college in California. That's what I am doing now. I drive to help pay the fees.'

'Your family must be quite well off to send you over here. How did you come? You must have connections.'

He grin at me in the rear mirrors. 'Not a penny. Not a single connection, apart from an older friend who was working here. I had twenty cents in my pocket when I arrived.'

I considered his new suit, a good tie, clean, perfectly ironed shirt. A certain opulence transpired from him.

'How long ago was this?'

'Three years ago. I slept on the floor in my friend's rented room for months. And, to survive, I cleaned toilets. A job no one wanted. I cleaned toilets for cash. I was not allowed to work, to start with.'

I was transfixed.

'And then?'

'And then, after months of cleaning loos, I started cleaning windows. I saved every penny.'

He looked at me in the mirror.

'From windows, I graduated to selling things in the street. Odd jobs. Whatever came up. It was not easy, but everything is possible in America.' He paused, there was pride in his voice.

'Now I have a green card. I go to college. I graduate next year.'

We were crossing many roads and finally went down the freeway towards Santa Monica. The ocean glittered, blue and turquoise, and on the white beach people jogged.

'It must have been hard to start with,' I murmured.

'Not really. I knew what I wanted to do and there is no work too humble, when you do it for a purpose.'

I loved that attitude.

'I work for an insurance company too. I study mostly at night and at weekends. Life is great.'

'Your family must be very proud of you back home.'

'They are. My brothers and sisters. Back in Kisumu.'

What a step from the busy, provincial little town on the shores of Lake Victoria to this chaotic modern symbol of America's metropolis.

'Do you miss Kenya?'

'I DO in a way. Yes. But I will go back next November. I saved enough for the ticket.'

I was more and more amazed, proud of him. He achieved the practically impossible.

We had reached Santa Monica. The ocean sparkled, small waves crowned in foam, and on the beach, walkman and headphones on, a young couple ran, holding hands. A few youths dashed fast amongst them rollerskating.

'Joseph' – he reminds me of another Joseph, the same joy in his eyes – 'Did you ever see an elephant back home in Kenya?'

I had managed to surprise him. For a moment his self-confidence was out of balance.

He braked, almost swerved.

'An elephant? Why?' His eyes were round with surprise. He shrugs.

And here, in his reaction, in his bewildered answer, was the drama of Africa's environment, the loss of identity of the African people, the reason why the environment is not safe, and my major reason for being in America.

To create awareness. To ask for help.

Local people in Africa cannot afford even to see their own wildlife. As if in Italy we could not afford to enter our churches, to be inspired by our monuments, to visit our museums, to contemplate the Roman ruins, to experience the art which makes Italy great. And this is why I have built the Wilderness Centre.

'An elephant? Of course not. How could I possibly see an elephant? How could I afford to see one?'

I have invited Joseph to come and stay in Laikipia when he returns to Kenya in the fall, to see the sun rise on the savannah in a deafening concert of birds, to walk to the waterfalls on the edge of the Great Rift Valley amongst palms and fig trees, and to stalk his first free elephant, king of the bush, so that when he returns to Los Angeles, the memory of the pachyderm which is part of his heritage will make him walk tall.

I know well that like thousands of other youths who have visited Ol ari Nyiro, he will never be the same, because he will have seen an elephant moving majestic and free through the African bush.

One Day, in Kiwayu

A man who is not afraid of the sea will soon be drowned,
he said, for he will be going out on a day he shouldn't.
But we do be afraid of the sea, and we do only be
drowned now and again.

J. M. SYNGE, *The Aran Islands*

The heat of the sand penetrated my tired body and I dug
my toes in it, stretching my muscles, content, finally relaxed,
conscious of having the whole earth as my bed. The sun
warmed my back. Through half-closed lids I could see the
small waves of low tide lapping the shore. The whiteness of
the beach reflected a million hidden crystals, minute shells,
and across the bay the island of Kiwayu was green, its lacy
acacia trees filigreed with hanging liana. The rocks encrusted
with oysters exposed by the tide were now rimmed with
foam, and a wind had begun to rise. Clouds were gathering
on the horizon: perhaps it would rain in the evening.

Today was my birthday, June the first, in Kenya Madaraka
Day, a national holiday. We had flown to this idyllic stretch
of sand not far from the Somali border on my return from
a long overseas trip. Here I could rest before going back to

my demanding work routine, get rid of the jet-lag, celebrate my birthday away from disturbances, thousands of kilometres far from civilization, where no telephone, no message could reach me. Even in Laikipia the problems accumulated during my absence would have been waiting for me. It had been Aidan's idea, thoughtful, caring as ever. Kiwayu was special to me.

A place full of memories of sand crabs dancing away on light legs, like my emotions, of small grey waves licking the shore, red suns melting on pearly waters, as in a floating mirror of coral and quicksilver. Of walking to the village of Mkokoni, where Paolo and I had once spent a blissful summer camping on the beach. Of Emanuele sailing out for cowries with the fishermen in the early morning, his thin arm lifted, waving goodbye. Of night picnics on the sand, sitting on large damp cushions of cotton *kangas*, smell of sea wind and long-gone youth.

I breathed the warm, balsamic sea-air deeply. Next to me, Sveva stood up.

'I have been asked to go out sailing. Can I?'

I looked at her long tanned legs, hips which had recently taken a new rounded shape, a body which seemed to have bloomed almost overnight, while I had been in America to launch my book, to talk for the Foundation, to work. She shook her heavy, honey-coloured mane of hair, one of her most striking features, and I realized with surprise that she was a child no longer. Gone was the chubby Mediterranean angel face, the fine silver gold baby-hair. Soon, any time now, she would be a woman. Soon she would be gone.

'Are you sure you know how to?'

With the sudden, resolute Paolo's look which I knew I could never fight, a determined glint in her oceanic eyes, she turned to me. A smile of full lips, Paolo's white teeth, the radiance of her glowing complexion.

'If I never try, I shall never learn. I'll be back for lunch.'

She ran off, a glimpse of youth and blonde and copper, to join her waiting friend. Only a short unease, a brief misgiving; and the tide of sleep and exhaustion, the giddiness of the jet-lag, the warmth and the rhythmic, hypnotizing sound of the ocean claimed me, and I was asleep.

I woke up slowly feeling stiff. My shoulders were burning and the sun was now over the zenith. I glanced at my watch and saw that I had been asleep for over two hours. I must get back to my thatched cottage, see how Aidan was, find Sveva. I was hungry now.

I stood and looked along the beach. A solitary figure was coming towards me, almost running.

The wind was stronger and the choppy sea looked green and murky, with large ugly waves heavy with seaweed.

I sheltered my eyes with one hand and saw that it was Aidan. His tall frame bent forward against the wind, he moved with a curious speed. There was a sort of urgency in his step which I could detect even at that distance. With a quickening in my heart I ran towards him. A greeting smile died on my lips when I saw his face.

He always came straight to the point. His voice was more serious than ever. Its gravity added to my apprehension.

'You'd better come quick. It's Sveva. There has been an accident. I am afraid she doesn't look too good.'

Instantly, my mouth dried out and my voice with it. A silent scream rose within me, from those depths of agony I had visited before, closing my throat, carrying, like a chill breeze, the familiar sense of horror, impotence and impending loss.

Not again.

Oh no. No. Not Sveva. Not Sveva, oh gods in heaven.

In moments of despair my soul goes begging to the spirit friends I have in the world of beyond. The ones I have loved and lost. The ones who would always care for my tears and for my pain.

Paolo, oh Paolo. Emanuele, Emanuele, please. Nonna, Nonna. Please. Not Sveva, please, not her.

I stood only an instant irresolute, a painful rigidity choking me. Aidan's blue eyes were slits of worry, his forehead closed in a frown. He held me up.

'. . . Not really serious. It's her eye. Her face. She was hit . . .'

I was running. Why was the burning sand so cold at high noon that day in Kiwayu under my flying feet? Why was the distance between me and the cottage in the raffia palm grove interminable? Why was the beating of my fear like a pulsating drum which deafened any other sound? And all along, in the back of my mind, the knowledge that it was now afternoon and a national holiday, that we were hours of flying from any medical help. We could never make it before dark.

Aidan could have flown in any weather, with any moon, but tonight there would be no moon at all. We could not fly in total darkness over lightless lands.

I prayed with no words to the ones who would care enough to make a difference.

Please please please Paolo, Emanuele, Nonna, per piacere aiutatemi.

The familiar, determined coolness which terror carries with it took hold of me again and I split in two. The other Kuki ran. The sun was dark and alien like a sun in the moon. *Run Kuki run.* The last rise over the last dune. A tangle of sea vines twisted around her ankle and almost tripped her over. The entrance of the room, sheltered by bright cotton *kanga.* The palm matting on the floor cool, soft under the soles of her feet. She held herself a moment against the door-frame, short of breath, and she was there. Back to the here and now, and to herself.

In the dark it took some moments for my sun-dazed eyes to adjust. Sveva lay on my bed, wrapped in a red wet *kanga.* The young man who had taken her out sailing was crouched at the bed's foot holding his head. Ignoring him, I ran to her, calling her name, and when she heard my voice she moaned.

She is alive. She is alive.

I looked.

Her wet hair was plastered to her skull. Below it, what had been her angel face was red and swollen, covered in blood. A crescent shaped open cut scarred her left cheekbone, and blood mixed with tears dribbled on my bed linen. She looked up at me through tears.

'I see two of you. I see two of everything. Mamma. Will I be all right?'

Since she was a little girl, when anything happened, a

scratch, a fever, a pain of any sort, with total faith she asked me: 'Will I be all right?' and waited for the verdict with an absorbed expression of complete trust.

My heart fluttered, at her reverting to childhood in a time of pain and need. She was alive, yet she might be disfigured. She could be blinded.

She moved and tried to sit. Her eyes rolled, I held out my hand in time to help her gently back to her pillow. She was suddenly sick. I took her in my arms trying not to touch her skin, giving the others quick instructions.

In the hurry of packing a small bag after arriving yesterday from the United States, I had forgotten to take my first-aid kit. There was no mercurocrome. No antibiotic cream. Nothing really but a harsh disinfectant that I knew would cook the skin badly, and butterfly plaster stitches that I knew I had to find the courage to use. Boiled water then; ice. The delicate skin below her eye should not be disturbed. Radiocall the hospital. Ask their advice. No question of having enough daylight hours to be able to make it back to Nairobi. And tomorrow would be too late for stitches.

'I can't see. I see double. Two of you. Two beds. Two Aidans. I feel sick. Sorry.'

She was sick again.

'Mamma. Mamma, will I be all right? Will I be able to see again?'

There had been narrow escapes before. The time she had been attacked by killer bees. The time her horse had bolted when she was pursuing zebra, and she had been catapulted into the rocks. The time that she, still a toddler, had refused to board the car already packed to go back to Nairobi from Laikipia. She had stopped in her tracks, unusually stubborn, ready to throw an uncharacteristic tantrum. It was Wanjiru who had told me to humour her.

'*Nyawera*,' she had said, calling me by my Kikuyu nickname, '*Makena najua. Kama yeye ataki hio ngari, lazima iko na kwa sababu.*' You, The One Who Works Hard, The One Who Smiles knows. If she does not like that car, there is a reason.

Reluctantly, I had moved all the luggage to a land cruiser. I felt the absurdity of the situation, but Sveva's and Wanjiru's coalition was too powerful to fight.

Next day, when our driver Karanja drove a friend who had been staying with me in Laikipia, to Nairobi in the other car, over the Kabete escarpment it lost a wheel which we did not know was loose. Out of control, the car flew over the bank, overturned and crashed, and my guest fractured her spine. I drive much faster than Karanja. The thought of what could have happened had we been in that car, dried out my saliva. Inscrutably, with the African acceptance of the improbable, Wanjiru had nodded.

'*Asante Makena*,' was all she said. Thank you, The One Who Smiles.

There had been the time that, during an evening walk with the dogs at Paolo's dam beyond Kuti, we had wandered without realizing it into the middle of a herd of elephants. They had been so silent that in the twilight I had not seen them. Unknowingly we had ended up almost between the legs of a towering matriarch invisible in the dusk. A sudden blare of trumpeting coming from a yard or so above us,

ivory tusks protruding, a huge head shaking, flared ears.
And in an instant I had gathered up Sveva, a child of four
or so, and had run at an angle towards the elephant, in the
direction of the wind, to get out of the line of scent as soon
as possible. My heart in my mouth, legs scratched by thorns,
trying to avoid the remaining herd, only after a while did I
realize that Sveva, bobbing up in my arms, was waving at
the elephant, giggling.

And there had been, of course, the time, soon after Emanuele's death, when a little friend had pushed her by mistake
into the swimming pool at Kuti, and run away in fear. She
had sunk to the bottom, a baby who could not yet swim, but
inexplicably she had managed to climb out alone, soaked,
but safe. There had been other stories. Accident prone, as
Paolo had been, there was however something unknown –
or someone invisible – which saved her in potentially tragic
situations, some benign force that had so far rescued her.

Now the story came amongst broken sobs, and it chilled me.

They had sailed out in the choppy sea with the irrespons-
ibility of youth, without life jackets. Sveva thought it would
be easy, thought her friend would know how. The current
of the receding tide took the small craft further and further
from the shore. There were no other boats to be seen. The
place was about to be closed for the Long Rains season, and
all craft had been taken ashore. Somehow I had been spared
the horror of watching, useless witness, impotent to intervene.
That would have maddened me. Sveva tried to grasp the
slippery side of the boat to keep her balance. Then the wind
caught the sail violently, the boom turned, hit her across the

face, flung her into the water. The boat capsized. Sky the colour of fright swirled above her eyes.

Stunned and unconscious she went under water, heavy as lead, but inexplicably she did not sink and bobbed up again. The cold made her regain consciousness and miraculously she managed to keep afloat, pain burning her face, eyes blinded with blood and salty water, waves higher and higher, and no life jacket. The aquatic Paolo streak prevailed in her as it had long ago, when she was pushed into the pool in Laikipia.

Yet again, when she could easily have drowned, she did not. The pain and the chill kept her conscious and she managed to stay afloat. Then the boy grasped a lock of her hair, floating like a bronze seaweed amongst the driftwood, and lifted her on the now righted boat, where she embraced the mast. Painstakingly, they reached the shore when Aidan, who was working at his papers in the cottage, was alerted by a boat attendant.

The afternoon drew on. Through the crackling of static, on the radio, the nurse in charge at the Casualty department at Nairobi Hospital gave us instructions, reassured us. We were to keep Sveva cool, quiet; give her pain-killers. Tomorrow we would leave at sunrise for Nairobi, and the hospital. But for today, only I could help.

I kept vigil over her agitated sleep, anxiously drying out oozing serum mixed with blood and praying that her face would be spared. When darkness fell I knew that the time had come for me to stitch the cut. It was drying out open, a gash shaped like a fan, and, unless I acted now, it would stretch her smooth skin and leave a nasty scar. Aidan held high the hurricane lamp and the young man a torch while I, conscious that it was up to me to keep her beauty, steadying my hands and biting my lips, applied the stitches to my girl's face one by one. From the swelling and pain I knew that her cheekbone was fractured. Perhaps the eye was affected. I finished finally. But she would not die.

Two years have gone by now and she is unblemished. The eye has finally recovered, and even if her eyesight has been slightly affected, the bone has mended and only a fine crescent shaped line, translucent like a new moon, remains below her left eye to remind us of that afternoon in Kiwayu.

The doctor next day commented that the stitches were applied perfectly; mother concern and love had guided my hands. But Sveva and I knew that it is the spirit friends who had helped again. Until next time.

Next time was a couple of years later, here in Laikipia, while she was driving with her friend Tim in a wave of music along the short cut between the Big Dam and the Wilderness Centre.

My large land cruiser climbed a steep slope too fast, landed sideways on the opposite downhill side and bounced up.

She hit the brakes, lost control, and the car rolled. She banged her head on the ceiling, and was catapulted like a rag doll stunned, unconscious, to the back of the vehicle. Driverless, the car kept going at full speed, rolled once more and landed on its roof. The front windscreen hit a jagged stump and exploded in a thousand crystals.

Shahar, the agriculturalist from Israel who had at that time just joined our team, was riding his bike towards the Centre, when he saw the car: upside down, the engine still running, music still pouring out and no one inside. The stump of an acacia branch, pushed against the front seat, would have beheaded her, had she still been in the driver's seat.

The car roof had caved in. A death trap.

The tracks of naked feet were visible in the red dust, and Shahar followed them.

She was walking in a daze, holding Tim's hand. She had crawled out of the window, extracted and comforted him. His collar bone was broken.

She did not have a single scratch.

Then there was the night in Nairobi a couple of years ago. It was her last day of school in Kenya before leaving to study in Europe. She had gone out to the end of year party.

I went to bed early and woke up suddenly in the middle of the night.

There had been a noise.

It had been raining earlier on but it had stopped now. Water dripped from the guttering. The dogs were silent. Someone was knocking, urgently, at the downstairs door.

'Mummy, open the door.'

I shook off the sleep.

'What happened to your keys ... it's four in the morning ...'

'Mummy, we've been robbed. They took everything. Open the door. I'm all right.'

Soaked in rain, her long hair damp on her shoulders, Sveva stood with her friend Tim on my doorstep. Over a steaming mug of tea the story unfolded.

Their car, moving slowly in the heavy rain, had been

ambushed up the hill, in Forest Road. A *panga* had gone through the half-lowered window, Tim had been yanked from the car and made to kneel on the grass at the side of the road. His face was pushed into a muddy puddle, a foot placed on his back to hold him down, while a bandit searched and robbed him. Sveva had crouched inside, invisible in the dark, protected by the fogged windows. With self-preservation she had removed from her neck her golden chain with the pendant of the two trees logo I had given her as a present. She hid it between her breasts and she got out. Caught unawares, the bandits turned. One leaped towards her, pushed her, took her purse, grabbed her blouse, began to undress her. Time stood still.

Smiling unexpectedly at angry, tense and frightened people disarms them, takes the wind from their sails, acts as a balm. It is often infallible and even this time it worked.

Standing in the night rain in deserted Forest Road, Makena bit her lip, swallowed her fear, smiled at the robbers, and joked with them in her fluent, gracious Swahili.

Could they not see that they were young, and there was nothing much they could get out of them, they had a little money, here it was, they could take her watch, here it is, take it, a good watch from Europe, and her necklace with blue lapis lazuli, it was real silver — you can always get another watch, another necklace — could they not see it was cold and they were wet, all they wanted to do was to go home?

The bandits were caught unprepared. They knew how to deal with rage, with fear, with aggression. Her calm, her words, her bright smile disarmed them.

73

Once again, the silent star of Makena's luck prevailed; another escape, as for Paolo, long ago. The page was turned, the time for violence gone, the robbers disappeared into the fog, like a nightmare at dawn.

The rain kept falling on the deserted road.

Looking for Sandy

In memory of Sandy Field

Great things are done when men and mountains meet.

WILLIAM BLAKE, *Gnomic Verses, i.*

The morning of the 14th of June 1996, dark clouds gathered in the sky over Nairobi, brought by strange and invisible winds. It had been one of Kenya's weirdest rainy seasons in people's memory.

The long rains of April had been delayed, and when finally the sky darkened one afternoon and large warm tears of water fell in untidy splashes, faster and faster on the parched red soil of my garden at Gigiri, we were well into May, in fact into June, almost.

In Laikipia the cattle had grown thin, and the Centre Dam was so low that, with a few shreds of meat, we could gather a bucketful of crayfish in a few minutes just from the shore.

The buffalo I met on the road at night stood dazzled in the car headlights. Rooted on stocky legs, with bent heads, the heavy horns weighing them down, the old males' muzzles lifted towards the car. Opaque ribs showed below dusty hides, a weariness in their eyes, and lions grew alert, I knew, waiting for their chance.

75

Through the dry sparse silver grasses, windswept in the evenings on the ridge of Mugongo ya Ngurue, I could see Lake Baringo shrink, the banks emerging, brown on the jagged shores; the middle island grew larger, accentuating its sleeping dinosaur shape; hiding in the muddy shallows where fish had long disappeared, hungry crocodiles began to attack goats, and the tree frogs were thirsty and silent in the chilly nights.

In Enghelesha, the fields that Shahar, our young agriculturalist from Israel, had prepared for planting, were waiting too; clouds came and went, bypassing us, and the sound of thunder filled the sky, grumbling only from the west over the Cherengani hills. The eastern sky, from where the rains come to Laikipia, remained clear and sparkling blue like wild convolvulus.

The lawn in my garden at Kuti dried partially, and Paolo's dam was empty, the creamy chocolate clay in the bottom cracking slowly in the sun.

The elephant waited for the night to settle before approaching my garden, tempted by the still green shrubs and fresh leaves on the irrigated parts; and the *askari* had a hard time restraining them from getting too close to the graves. Their dung was found practically every morning, still steaming, all along my drive, and as close as Sveva's old playroom. Often buffalo and zebra droppings began to appear too, closer and closer on the murram paths, and my dogs howled their disdain at the renewed invasion of their territory, but their barks were lost in the moonless nights with the cries of plovers.

The concert of birds, converging from miles around to

the bird baths and the pawpaw that we laid out on the stones for them, took over any other sound in the scorching afternoons. Hundreds, thousands of birds, covering the dogs' food bowls with an incessant flutter of feathers.

Then, from the garden taps came a gasping sound, and we knew that the water had dried out in the tanks, and we had no choice but to pump it all the way from Ol ari Nyiro springs, well over six miles away.

There was no grazing left; only below the *lelechwa* did some grass sprout still, grey with age and exhausted of life. Even my rain stick did not seem powerful enough this time to stir the clouds.

Finally, brought to despair, I decided to follow the ancient custom of the land, and hired some old *wazee* from Mutaro to perform a rain ceremony. A sheep was found, completely black, with no white markings whatsoever, and, led by Garisha, a cattleman from Meru whom we had employed on the ranch for years, the old men sang and danced below an old *mugumu* tree next to the Mukutan stream, slaughtered the sheep ceremonially, and proceeded to consume in secret, ritually but with satisfied glee, certain chosen parts.

We waited. We waited hoping to hear the sound of rain on the roof and the frogs waking up in the pond. But nothing seemed to happen.

About a week had gone by when, although no apparent change was detected in the air by us humans, bees started swarming, passing above the yellow fever trees in buzzing clouds which cast fast shadows. On the newly potted palms, on the papyrus in the fish pond, the weaver birds landed to tear off long shreds and, in a frenzy of activity, they began nesting. Soon, heavy bunches like intricate baskets festooned the acacias' branches on the west side of the wind, and my cook Simon took to looking east, with straight head and wide nostrils sniffing the air, and commenting gravely: '*Mimi nasikia arufu ya mvua.*' I can smell the rain.

Then I woke up one morning, and knew that the wind had stopped. The air had grown moist, pregnant with water, and the heavy western sky purple and black. Clouds hung, lead coloured, gathering above like a moving blanket.

Thunder and lightning shook the sky, a sudden breeze lifted, the bougainvillaea trembled, livid in the strange grey light, and the rains came.

In Laikipia the termites woke up from their secret tunnels, the earth opened, and golden clouds of living insects drifted high in the last twilight of dusk, in a nuptial frenzy of new wings, dancing dizzily upward.

They did not seem to stop. The dams filled and overflowed; the Mukutan stream became a river, hurling down the *luggas* and the gorge with a continuous roar. The Demu ya Schule had gone over the road, the gap filled with murky water widened, and the Wilderness School woke up as an island on a livid morning of more incumbent water. The staff, the following night, all standing in their nightdresses on the tables and desks, had to be rescued urgently because the level kept mounting and no one could swim. The land cruiser which went over to fetch them never got out of the water, and we had to send a tractor next day to tow it. Cars got stuck continually in the black cotton soil, and in the gluey red clay alike, and everywhere was flooded.

Crayfish became impossible to catch, now that the Centre

Dam had become a mighty lake, refilled constantly by the Big Dam, and, after subsequent showers formed countless running streams, a constant flow of water ran from the overflow, to concentrate into a deafening, rumbling grey river billowing through the valley of Maji ya Nyoka. There is no mid-way in Africa: it is either drought or floods, life or death, it is the land of opposites.

All our rain-catchments were full as they had not been in years. Our sixty-two dams were unrecognizable.

The Red Dam, the Black Dam, Nagiri's Dam and Ngobithu's Dam, were fuller than they had ever been. And Mutamayo Dam, Nandi Dam, Enghelesha Dam, Corner Dam, Luoniek Dam, Ol Morani Dam, Kudu Dam and Dam ya Faru had flooded over the road; new islands had emerged everywhere, water ran into the *lelechwa*, waterbucks stood confused on the flooded shores. Even water holes were enormous.

In the kitchen at Kuti a few inches of muddied water covered the floor, where Simon waded ankle-deep and barefooted, rolling croissants impassively, with great style.

In Nairobi, it became a problem to take off and to land in the dense fogs; and often the airfields at Wilson were closed to any traffic for hours.

It was a morning like this, the one of June 14th. I had taken off at 12 p.m. with Benjamin Woodley, our pilot and game warden, who had come to fetch me with our plane.

The clouds hung low; a grey impenetrable curtain covered the Aberdares. We circled round the clouds, going too far south in the process, well off our north-west route. We flew very low, with no shadow, over herds of goats, which streamed away like brown and white seeds scattered on the flat savannah by a hurried hand. Masai herdsmen clad in red blankets looked up, leaning on their spears, so close I could see the colour of their beads and the knots of their *rungus*, and when, beside the cattle, I began to see giraffe and zebra, I knew that we had gone well below the Longonot crater. We circled and circled, first lower, then higher, trying to find an opening in the barrier ahead. But the sky looked ominous, closed to our probing.

We climbed finally above the clouds, so high that my fingertips became dizzy and my head too light, and I found it hard to keep my eyes open in the blinding white reflection of spun clouds and the sun, too close and too aloof to care for us daring insects. I felt unimportant and vulnerable, suspended in a man-made flying machine inadequate to compete with such powers.

Yet we managed to make it. Benjamin, skilled and cool-headed, finally located a hole in the canopy and dived through the sky as a fish into the deepest ocean; found a gap through the cliffs of Hell's Gate, and we flew very low over the siphons of hot smoking sulphur. Some large buffalo crouching on the grass looked up at us; waterbuck and eland and giraffe and zebra galloped off, but there before us Lake Naivasha glimmered, pale yellow reflections rimmed the clouds announcing tentative sunshine ahead, and we aimed towards it, past Ol Bolossad, up the escarpment.

Far on the right we left the dark Wanjohi area of deep forest and bamboo and igenia, black in a storm of rain.

I looked ahead at the familiar hills on the Great Rift.

Enghelesha, Kutwa, Mugongo ya Ngurue. It was the Laikipia plateau, and with immense relief I knew we were safe.

At the same time our friend Sandy Field, piloting his Cessna 172, was disappearing to his destiny somewhere, perhaps in the bamboo and cedar forest, perhaps crashed over the waterfalls, where he may never be found again.

Sandy Field was a man of adventure and charisma, had been a gallant soldier and competent administrator. As a young man he was posted to Sudan, and spoke many local languages fluently. Brave in the bush, where he shot big game, in control and at ease at social gatherings, he had a flair for words, an amazing memory and an extensive repertoire of quotations and poetry. Old fashioned, cultured, polished, slim and white-haired, with a witty smile, he was a great old gentleman, entertaining and fun to be with.

Now in his seventies, he still flew his small plane every-where, and was regarded as a cautious, competent pilot.

On the ranch in Laikipia, without a telephone, and having neglected for a few days to listen to the sked on the Laikipia Security radio network, I did not know what had happened. I heard nothing until I flew back to Nairobi a few days later; there, at Wilson Airport in the early morning, I saw a group of Highlands friends leaning against their plane with steaming mugs in their hands, unshaven, silent, wearily eating sandwiches out of a box, sitting on one wing next to some open maps.

'Having a picnic breakfast? What's the occasion?'

The question hung in the air, and then Will answered.

'We are looking for Sandy.'

'Sandy?'

'He flew out of Wilson last Friday for Nanyuki. He never landed. Everyone who has a plane is looking. We have subdivided the area on a grid system. It is going to be tough, but we are trying to find him.'

But it was more difficult than we had all anticipated.

In any other country perhaps, finding a person missing in a storm with his airplane would have been a problem left to the authorities. But not in Kenya. Here the solidarity and friendship that unites the people of the Highlands once again prevailed, and everyone who had a plane or could hire one went looking for Sandy.

I felt I too had to do my share. I liked Sandy. I admired his intelligence, his agile mind, his wit. I respected his courage and leadership. Like his friend Wilfred Thesiger, he was one of the few remaining old soldiers of bygone days, with the soul of a poet, the manners of a gentleman. Kind, eloquent, witty, a strong personality, an addition to every party, quality and humour exuded from Sandy. His disappearance left us all bewildered.

We searched for days and then weeks. Whenever we flew, even after everyone had given up hope of finding him, I kept looking down the secret valleys, the steep walls of rock, the thickets of bamboo and cedar in the hope of finding a sign. But in vain.

All the wildest stories, the most adventurous guesses soared and subsided after a while. Sandy had flown south to Tanzania; had disappeared in the Naivasha Lake; had crashed on Mount Kenya; was alive, in Ethiopia. The last word on the radio before silence had been 'Abyssinia'. We would find him alive up Mount Meru, camped below the wing of his plane . . .

During the search, an old propeller airplane, of whose remote disappearance there was no record, was discovered on the bottom of Lake Naivasha; countless illegal charcoal kilns had been reported, and logging of the rare, precious igenia in unvisited forests, but no trace of Sandy.

Still, we looked from the plane, scanning every crag of the mountains. And then a medium from Europe declared that the plane had gone down in a certain gorge of the Aberdares next to the Wanjoi valley, and, to clear our conscience, we decided to go and look.

We left at sunrise from Laikipia, Aidan and I, on a dark morning of late June, and drove, through muddy tracks, up green hills and mountains. At the park gate we took with us a ranger who knew the way, a young Tugen from our boundary of Enghelesha, it transpired, trim and fit, well equipped with rucksack and tentage, and a very good uniform. We got stuck a few times up hill, walked in the red mud to put branches below the wheels and were astonished to see so many tracks of lions and hyena spoor. I wondered what they ate, as there seemed to be few signs of buck.

Lions were not indigenous to the Aberdares. They had been recently introduced, and – ecological tragedy – had multiplied beyond balance, almost completely destroying the rare and shy bongo antelope that feeds on the moss growing off fallen trees in the cold and rainy mountain slopes. In recent times, drawn by hunger, they had been known to attack and kill people, and I knew a scheme to control their numbers was under way.

Finally, we reached a fog-covered peak, where for short seconds when there was a break in the clouds, a sensational landscape intermittently appeared below us. We set camp at dusk, in the middle of the track, as the sides were thick with impenetrable vegetation. There was a drizzle of rain which soon grew to a mighty downpour; every inch of tent was wet and the mattress was swimming in chilled water. We ate a scalding bowl of soup, and piping hot stew to revive us, cooked on a small camping gas-stove that I had providently brought, for our campfire would not burn with wet wood, and, after a hot, sweet rum punch, we slept surprisingly well.

In the morning the search began down the crags of the land, over the slopes and inside the bamboo thickets. But it was in vain, and at night we finally returned, convinced that Sandy would never be found.

The bamboo, we knew, would have closed, resilient, over the plane and would have grown many feet in few days, obliterating it from view for ever.

Everyone knew that the forest was full of wild animals, and hyena are unkind to the wounded and weak. We hoped for a quick end, a peaceful rest in the unknown forest grave.

In *absentia cadaveris*, a memorial service was celebrated for Sandy in the church in Nanyuki, resplendent with elaborate flower arrangements by the accomplished ladies of the Gardening Club. There was all the crowd one sees at weddings and at funerals, at the polo matches of the North Kenya Polo Club, and at the Beating of the Retreat in Nanyuki, when some kilted Scottish battalion marches back and forth in the drizzle, with impeccable martial choreography, to the lament of Highland pipes. Everyone knew everyone else, all men wore identical blue blazers over ill-fitting trousers, the women assorted frocks and flowery hats. There were old settlers, farmers and retired game wardens, old timers and, finally visible, the faceless voices of the Laikipia Security Network.

Sandy's friends delivered moving eulogies, like Tony Dyer, a fellow pilot and a contemporary, and few eyes were dry. Everyone sadly agreed that we would never know where Sandy lay.

But we were wrong.

The honey gatherers found him.

They had been up in the forest slopes, smoking out bees from the old olive trees across the clumps of bamboo. They heard thunder meeting earth, and the shudder of the impact. They ran towards it, warily at first, and then, spying through the dripping leaves, they saw it, the white bird of metal that had fallen from the clouds and crashed miserably, a wounded seagull, sinking through the tall green foliage like a boat at sea.

They watched breathless for a while to see what happened, what creature would erupt from the contorted wreck. There was only silence, except for the shrill calls of invisible monkeys up on the treetops, the sound of water rushing from the bamboo.

In the impact, Sandy's life had lifted from his body and joined what was before, and after. Over the purple-ink clouds of the Great Rift, gliding along the waterfall's drops covered in moss, over the silent lakes bejewelled with flamingos, over the valleys and savannah, riding on the long necks of giraffes galloping in slow motion on the plains, or amongst trumpeting elephants in the dust, up on the mountain slopes and up up to the dazzling light of the equatorial sun, like a butterfly finally hatching from its cocoon, what had been Sandy's energy, now freed from his body, exploded to blend with the Whole.

The men approached tentatively, climbed over the wing and spied inside: the *musungu* reclined on the steering wheel, his white hair visible, his forehead resting on the dashboard splintered in a thousand diamonds of exploded glass. He looked asleep, but the two men knew with the wisdom of the bushmen, from the shape of the neck, that the white man would never move again.

There was no harm, they thought, to find what he had no longer use for – clothes, watch, shoes, money perhaps? – that they could well use. It had been a bad year; life was hard on the mountain. The last honey harvest had been meagre and it looked as if the next one would be too. What if they helped themselves to what would rot anyway up the mountain?

No one would suffer and no one would find out. They cut the seat belt and dragged him out of the plane. He was light. Gently – there was no hurry – they put him on his side, and searched his clothes. They worked quickly, without talking, taking everything they could. His briefcase, all his clothes, his shoes. Then they covered the wreck of the plane with branches to hide it from the sky, for even in their ignorance they knew there would be a search. The more delayed the finding, the more chances they had of not being found. The forest animals would come. It would be easy, quick. Hyena were always pacing the game trails at night with their loping gait, sniffing for food. The forest would swallow the *musungu* man as it was now swallowing them, thick, impenetrable, keeper of secrets.

Loaded, happy they ran off, the honey search forgotten for today, to divide the loot in a safer place.

But it was not the hyena.

When the night came with its cloak of fog and drizzle up on the mountain slopes, and the night frogs woke up in a choir of life, the old leopard came out of its den under the boulder of rock, hung with fern and wild figs.

The leopard sniffed the air and moved slowly and surely through the undergrowth, towards the strange white shape in the bamboo.

And it was the leopard who carried Sandy off to the tall tree.

The forest men, months later, having learned of the reward offered for Sandy's discovery, went to report to the nearest forest station. A group of friends in the helicopter lent by Halvor Astrup went to land immediately on that spot, which no plane or car could have reached. Traces of hair on the dashboard and the cut belt told their story, and so did the leopard spoor abundant round the wreck.

Now Sandy lives in a leopard up the mountain slopes, a healthy strong lustrous leopard, and we know that he would have loved that.

The Road to Rubu

We shall not cease from exploration
And the end of all our exploring
Will be to arrive where we started
And know the place for the first time.

T. S. ELIOT, *Little Gidding*

One summer, not so long ago, we decided to go north of
Kiwayu to explore, Aidan and Sveva and I. We bought
a second-hand Land-rover old enough not to represent a
temptation to *shiftah*,* but in good enough condition to carry
us safely with the luggage and camping kit that we had
purchased. Aidan also acquired a boat, a sturdy white plexi-
glass dinghy with an awning to shelter us from the sun, a
good engine, and a spare engine, which had been Paolo's,
kept safe in a store in my house at Kuti, where it had waited
for years, for the time when again it may feel the same
waters.

The plan was to drive north of Kiwayu, cutting a track
along the overgrown trails to Rubu, on the north Kenya

---

* Bandits from Somalia or Ethiopia.

coast. This was an area which, for over a generation, no one had gone through because of the constant threat from bandits roaming the lands near the Somali border, around the frontier town of Kiunga.

I had journeyed there first in the summer of 1973, when Paolo and I, young, in love and eager to explore remote corners of the country we had just chosen as our home, had travelled north with our car and a rubber dinghy, and spent two magical weeks in a tent pitched on the beach at Mkokoni.

To reach it we had driven through barren and untamed country, encountering wild animals, visiting small Muslim villages and making friends with the people. With our boat we had glided happily round the canals and climbed up steep tangled slopes, spotting wildlife on the sandy dunes covered in sea vines, and marvelling at the rare privilege of discovering that so much virgin, unspoiled land still existed, it seemed to us then, for us alone.

So it was, to some extent, to retrace our steps, that I returned twenty-three years later, and found that very little had changed.

The elephants were no longer there, belly-deep in the tidal ponds, and the blue waterlilies had died out. But we saw a cheetah the first day, and lesser kudu and dik-dik at the side of every track.

We drove into Mkokoni first, looking for Mote, the fisherman Paolo and I had employed that long-lost summer, more than twenty years ago.

He had been a young man then, nimble of body, quick

to spot fish in the shallows, agile and ready to steer his boat through the labyrinth of mangroves of which he knew every turning. In those two weeks we had shared adventures, and, with unfailing generosity, he had put himself and all his competence at the service of these two young *wasungu*, the first to come so far through dangerous and unvisited country, and to stay on.

Over the years I had not forgotten him, and I had seen him once in the late seventies during one of Emanuele's half terms, when an exclusive safari village for discerning guests had been built along our beach, and I went to find some of my memories and him.

Emanuele had loved to collect cowries in those days, and Mote promptly offered his *maho** and two of the crew to sail out of the Melango at high tide and wait for the tide to go out, exposing the bank of molluscs at Oyster Bay, where, with luck, a *Cipraea Vitellum* or perhaps *Caput Serpentis* could be found, to my son's delight.

I had not seen Mote since, and was not sure if he was still alive: after all, Paolo and Emanuele had died, wiped out by an indifferent destiny, and the life of a fisherman in the Indian Ocean is not a long one: his brother had been eaten by a shark, while diving for lobster just out of the Melango.

But Mote was still there.

He came in from the beach where he had been fishing, a loincloth round his belly, a live lobster glistening in his hand, still dripping wet and with the light step I remembered, small

---

* A smaller version of a *daho*; traditional wooden sailing boat used by fishermen in the North Coast.

wizened face, and the slight figure of an old child. He looked up at us searchingly, and his face split almost instantly in a delighted grin.

Years ran like sand through the hourglass of his memory, and I knew he had remembered me.

'Allah Hakbar! Mama Kuki! Kwisha rudi! Leo mimi nafra. Nashukrani kubwa sana kwa Mungu.' May God be praised. Mama Kuki is back. I rejoice today and give thanks to God.

He intoned these words in a high-pitched voice, jubilant, and his cries soon attracted half the village. His brother Haji came out, bearded, older seemingly, fatter, greyer, resembling our Mote not at all: by another wife, I wondered?

Bajuni children and beautiful women assembled, colourful and elegant, greeting us. Soon we were sitting in the shade of Mote's house, on the Swahili beds of thatched doum-palm leaves, and were offered *tangawezi chai*,* with no milk. It was the full 'travellers' welcome', traditional in this strict Muslim community. Shelter, drink, food. Small sweet yellow corn cobs were produced for us, while we told of our safari and of what we wanted to do. A young man was recruited from the village, and our boat on its trailer was examined by everyone, found good enough, and accepted.

It took us three days to reach Rubu.

The village had been abandoned over twenty years ago, when constant *shiftah* incursions from neighbouring Somalia made it impossible for the inhabitants to stay on.

The track had become overgrown, tangled with liana,

---

* Ginger tea.

sansevieria and thorny acacia shrubs which scratched deep ridges on the car's metal, impeding our progress. But Aidan was determined, and with Mote, Ali the boatman and our young recruit, plus the drivers we had brought with us, we managed to clear a large enough gap for the vehicle to proceed slowly. We camped at night in the middle of the track – hooking mosquito nets on bushes over our mattresses – so dense was the vegetation around us that there was no room for our tents.

The bleached bones of an old elephant marked a spot, below five tall baobabs, where the entrance of Rubu had been. There were the crumbled ruins of a mosque. Small heaps of porous, decaying coral rocks indicated where houses had once stood, and disintegrating wells, made of yellow sand and lime. Arab inscriptions from the Koran, engraved on a few oval tombstones planted around with blue lilies, discovered behind a dune, indicated where the Rubu community had once laid their dead to rest. To one side, still partially functioning, was a flat *jabia*, the ingenious traditional way to collect rainwater to drink.

Sand vines and sansevieria grew everywhere, and on the slim stretch of grey beach left open by the mangroves, hundreds of fragments of broken crockery were scattered, blue and white and green and maroon, amongst pearly nautilus shells, and old elephant molars, yellowed with age and salt water: all that remained of a living community, already as ancient as millennia's old archaeological ruins. Far in the distance, over the bay, lay a long island, and the Indian Ocean glittered, breaking on the distant coral reef in sprays of white.

We cleared a patch over the sand dunes, and there we pitched our camp. The sound of the waves on the reef was unchanged.

The boat was lowered into the water next day, amongst singing, and *dahos* came over from the island to greet us; fishermen offered gifts of lobster and fish and left in a wake of songs and drums in the evening light.

Time seemed to stand still on the shores of Rubu, facing the long island which changes its names to match the names of the villages along the shore. It was a time of peace and harmony, of exploring the untouched shores where Muslim tradition had sheltered the people from the pollution of so-called progress, and lives still developed following ancient rhythms and customs.

The women were tiny, gracious, slim as girls, wrapped in bright *kangas* and with their hair plaited in smart, tight patterns; their ears were bright with red stones, the slender arms with bracelets, the small hands and feet painted with henna in floral motifs; sometimes a ruby glinted in a nostril, while barefoot children clung to their skirts.

They did not cover their faces, the Bajuni girls, like the Arab women in Lamu or Malindi, nor their heads, and I never saw them wearing a *buibui*, the black flowing, nun-like garment of the strict Muslim ladies of the Coast.

They looked at us from the shadows of their doors, shyly returning our greetings in sing-song voices; and curly-haired little girls stood next to them, enveloped in faded European-style frocks a few sizes too large, but with shiny, eager eyes, devoured by curiosity at our foreign appearance, by the details of our clothes and hair.

I have always been conscious of the scrutiny of those young eyes in Africa, when, at remote villages, the crowd of silent, observing children approaches. Drawn by curiosity they leave the repetitive monotony of the games they have been playing in the dark shade of their homes, assemble at a distance, and finally come close to your car, almost touching it, and there they stop, girls with girls and boys with boys, barefoot, slim, staring silently, absorbing everything, examining the foreign animals we are.

We went for long trips on the boat, circling the islands and waving when we met the fishermen's *dahos* cutting the waves, loaded with biblical figures in long *shukas*, turbans loosened by the monsoon. We slid beside cliffs of steep rocks, hung about with liana and wild aloes and sansevieria, with the odd baobab suddenly appearing silver and majestic through the undergrowth; we spotted awesome sculptures of driftwood on the beaches, carved by the endless fantasy of long waves, and once, a large iguana crouched precariously on the edge of a rock, grasping a branch protruding on the canal, her black tongue flickering, her glassy eye expressionless. A prehistoric encounter. We watched troupes of vervet monkeys taking over the dusk, jumping with incessant chatter amongst the baobab branches along the shore, where the small, black, left-handed crabs with one giant orange claw scurried down their holes in coordinated shifts, like dancers. We searched for oysters, with an old rusty hammer, and ate them where we were, half-submerged in the tidal ponds, squeezing a lime on their pearly flesh. We went bottom-fishing with Mote as I had once done with Paolo, and caught the same type of little round fish, silver-pink, with a black spot on the side, which Mote roasted for us on the beach on a rudimentary spit cut out of a fresh mangrove twig, and which we ate with our hands, skin and all.

While trailing with our boat in the evenings, we sometimes caught some very large red snapper and Aidan's surprised joy was like a child's, endearing in the experienced man that he is. We cooked them whole, with spices, lime juice and garlic; our camp was lovely, with large, open mess tents like verandahs, and two Lamu beds for sofas, that Mote's brother had made for us on commission, and sold us for far too much.

It was extremely hot, but there blew an evening breeze, the moon rose creating strange shadows, and we were merry.

Over those days of bliss and simplicity, far from the noise and cares of a distant world, the idea slowly formed of finding a place somewhere in that area for us to come and unwind during the busy year, and, in exchange, to start some activity to benefit that community. Something to protect the environment and to give people a way of life.

We sent messages.

So, the day came of the historical meeting of the *wazee*, who had travelled from far to hear what we had to propose.

From the beach, from the tracks overgrown with sea grapes, they began to come. They had heard from the fishermen's drums that we had opened again the old road to Rubu, these crazy *wasungu* who travelled by air, but had reached that spot by driving through harsh thorny land, and had pitched their camp on the beach, next to the mangrove bay, below the ruins of the house that had been Mohamed Mussa's.

The news had travelled at night, brought by rhythm and by song. Above the mangrove forests and clumps of doum-palms, through the tall tamarind trees and the outcrops of coral rocks overgrown with green creepers, to the pockets of people still living in clusters from Kiwayu to Kiunga, as far as Mkowe, through the fishermen's camps on the island, people listened and learned of this strange and unusual fact.

They knew that we travelled with Mote, *mχee* Mote from Mkokoni, and that we had hired Haji's son Ali. Some of them had already heard, when they were consulted for the spelling in Arabic of the word 'Rubu', painted in ocean-blue on the white side of the boat. And from Mkokoni to Kiwayu village they all could see Mote beaming with anticipation and growing in importance in his own eyes because of the association with us. From his behaviour alone they had guessed some excitement and novelty lay ahead. Who were these *wasungu*?

Everyone knows that *wasungu* are slightly touched: those who can sleep in beds and sit comfortably inside, but choose incomprehensible hardship, like walking for miles in the sun following camels, without being obliged to do so, or who sleep out in the open under a mosquito net in lion-infested areas, and come all the way to this god-forsaken land, remote from man and civilization, not a *duka* for hundreds of miles, not even a road to get there. And what for?

I presume it was an irresistible curiosity to find out why, and the concern that we might have some sort of plot for Rubu: they wanted to claim the place for theirs, as it was; to show that they had first stake, that they cared what went on there, even if for thirty years none of them had taken up a *panga*, called for companions and, slashing at the vegetation, for about fifteen miles, made their way through tse tse country on the old road to Rubu. Now the track had been opened and the spell was broken.

Speculations of all sorts were born each morning and died with each sunset, to be reborn at sunrise and discussed all day long. But now they had gathered to hear from us directly.

Alerted to the arrival of the wise men, Aidan had driven to Kiunga earlier, to fetch Chief Jamal, the DO and the assistant chief.

I served everyone *bajuni* tea, and biscuits, under the awnings of blue and turquoise *kangas*, and then they all gathered under the tamarind tree below the *jabia*. After a moment's hesitation, I declined Aidan's invitation to join them because this was a Muslim world and my presence at the start would have made them uneasy: I knew women did not appear unless called. I felt that, by this show of instinctive respect of their tradition, I would myself gain in respect, and this was auspicious. As it happened, shortly after the meeting began they sent for me, and it was a prouder thing to join them at their request than to sit there uninvited at a meeting in their own land.

The meeting began with prayers to Allah. They then spoke formally in turn, welcoming us amongst them, asking what they could do for us. They had been impressed by our determination to reach that spot, and at our respectful way of proceeding; they had learned that we were looking at the land and wanted to know what we had in mind. There were some old men, and some others quite young, whose wisdom had given them seniority. They sat cross-legged on the sand, dressed in clean long *kikois* and shirts, all wearing embroidered Muslim caps, apart from the DO who was a

Christian from Nandi, Mr Towett Maritim. He was still quite young, and very agreeable. Slim with an open, intelligent face, he was gifted with a positive attitude and natural leadership. He spoke very well, in excellent Swahili as they all do, in a sing-song of coastal accent, very pleasant to hear, the melodious intonation of all fishermen dialects across the world: a tone and a *cantilena* pitched to cover and pierce the sound of waves, to call from boat to boat over the oceans.

We told them of our love for that land, and of my memories of long ago; we explained our busy lives and our many commitments, but also our desire to find a place of quiet and peace, and of our intention – should they agree with our offer – to help them to rebuild and develop their village in a way that respected their old customs and their environment.

I looked at Aidan over the crowd of elders: another commitment, I could read in his eyes, with all the thousand things that already crammed our days. Yes, *wasungu* are mad, why ever start all again from the beginning, pioneering far from our known lifestyle, and our comforts?

But they listened with deep interest. We represented hope and change, adventure and challenge. Their eyes lit up, Allah was again invoked, they shook our hands repeatedly, they asked us to look around and to give them our proposed terms.

It took quite a while – like all things of worth – subsequent visits, letters, meetings in darkened offices in the old Lamu town, under palm-trees in the dusty town of Kiunga, in banks with fans whirring from ceilings of peeling plaster, and in open fields of cassava, where we managed to land to meet one more of the old people and get his blessing too: the unavoidable bureaucracy which is the other face of most dreams.

But finally, it was nearly done. Through my enthusiasm and Aidan's perseverance, his knowledge of the rules and his fairness of play.

It was for me the crowning of a dream long shared with Paolo, but which there had been no time to accomplish, to have the use of some land at the coast, and some sort of dwelling there, built to please the eye. Somewhere where the noise of the waves on the reef was the last sound at night and the first in the morning, a rhythmic, heaving sound like the beating of a large heart.

The image of Paolo kept coming back in that place he had loved most. Then we would sit and listen for the roar of lions, in the nights of those two lost weeks. And above the noise of the waves on the reef, brought by the *Kaskazi* wind from the sandy acacia-dotted savannah below the baobabs, sometimes we heard, with a shiver, the powerful deep call which is so much the sound of Africa.

Memories glided back with the tides at Rubu, when I paused on the shore, alone, to think, like waves reaching out on the grey sand between the mangrove sprouts.

Memories of Paolo.

Buffalo had enthralled him above all other African animals.

There, to his emotion, we watched a few old males coming down one evening to wet their muzzles in the semi-sweet brackish water amongst the mangrove.

Paolo.

Where was the shadow on the dunes, the tall slender shadow of the man who has gone? Why could we not say our farewells?

The long wait for him to come home, his voice on the telephone, disembodied, far away, then the shade growing longer on the lawn, a gloom descending with dusk, the intuition of loss, the ultimate pain, the startling agony of bewildered, foreseen loneliness, the knowledge of nevermore. I put my hands around my stomach, felt the life I was carrying, knew the other life had gone on. I knew there would be no more holding hands, eyes gleaming with life and excitement, deeply searching mine in a quest of love.

'Farewell' – I thought – 'my Paolo, Paolo of the golden hair, Paolo the chivalrous squire.'

And Paolo had left when his time was up. His time was up and there was nothing anyone could do. Circumstances, delays, a variety of events, brought Paolo to that spot where, at the same time, the faceless lorry-driver chosen by destiny decided to turn into Hunter's Lodge. And it was at Hunter's Lodge that Paolo the hunter met the trailer, when his time was up.

I knew it with a jolt which left me breathless. An abrupt intake of breath, as if his spirit, abruptly freed from the cage of its body, had exploded with the same powerful energy of when he was physically there.

And Paolo touched my face with his fingerless hands, caressed my stomach where his hidden child curled, slowly growing into the blonde, radiant Paolo-girl he would never see. The one who was now running towards me on the beach, long-limbed, suntanned, laughing.

Memories.

Memories of running uphill, sitting on windswept rocks at the moment of sunset, when there is a chill in the breeze, shivers run from the shoulders down, and we look at the lake, at the blue

Cherengani hills, at clouds with strange shapes, like dragons or fish. Of running downhill, hand in hand, eyes in the eyes, tripping on stones, and laughing.

Memories of long nights of music, the fire blazing, talking and talking.

Of other dogs sleeping on carpets, of other flowers fading away in vases.

Memories of brown, warm eyes, intelligent and old, even if young. A solitude, a far-away wisdom.

My lost child, my lost boy child.

In the months following our first visit we returned to explore with new eyes, no longer passing visitors who might never return; eager to find a good landing strip, slowly driving our boat up through the sleepy mangrove-lined canals at high tide. We discovered it at last, at a corner of the canal bordered by banks of red earth, below a hill crowned with baobabs and filigreed with porcupine tracks, the perfect landing strip. Bleached mangroves, like ancient noble bones exposed to salt and sun, lined the sides, and there Aidan landed his plane with ease.

It was late afternoon, almost sunset. Just enough time before darkness fell to pitch our tent beside the plane, gather a pile of firewood and light a fire to bake bananas and to boil water for tea. Fireflies danced in the warm night and from the coastal forest came the calls of bush-babies dancing high in the baobabs.

The following morning, leaving the plane on the shore, our tent and equipment a few metres from it, we jumped into our waiting boat. Mote left us on the beach, at Ndoa, and went to have his *chai* at the fishermen's camp on the island. We walked inland, exploring, following tracks of bush-pigs, and to our amazement saw a male bush buck jumping, alert and handsome, through the tangle of sea vines.

We went down to the sea to swim and, in a grotto left open for us by the receding tide, we set our picnic.

We were eating cold fish with lime and soya, when we saw Mote sprinting towards us. He leaped over the rocks, agile and lithe like a sand crab, and he was screaming. The ocean wind took away his words, and only when he was close we heard:

'*Moshi! Ni moshi mingi kwa campi yetu. Moto! Ni moto kwbwa . . . Ndege . . .*' Smoke. A big smoke in our camp. Fire. A large fire . . . the plane . . .

We already were running before he had finished. Gathering our gear, wading into the water up to our armpits, climbing into the boat, firing the engine. With a wide circle the boat gained the entrance of the *melango*, left the ocean boiling behind, reached the lagoon where the horizon spread before us. Standing on the rolling boat and sheltering our eyes with our hands, we watched in silence.

High into the sky, lifting exactly from the place we knew as Abukari – where, hidden behind the mass of green leaves, we had pitched our camp and our airplane was parked with all we had brought – over the mangrove forest, moving into the wind, ugly with the inevitable, lead-grey colour of fear, was an enormous column of smoke. No one spoke.

In the distance, running up and down the short beach at Rubu, we could see the small figure of Mohamed Mussa gesticulating towards us, urging us to hurry. The tide was

out, the water low, exposing banks of white sand, and there
was no way our boat could reach the bend in the canal and
the airstrip. We had to walk.

We jumped into the water before reaching the beach and
dashed off. Mohamed led the way. We flew uphill over the
sand dunes and reached the swamp. The forest closed over
our heads. The mangrove roots stood out, caked in mud,
like gigantic spiders. I tripped a few times, losing my sandals.
The sucking noise of crabs and raucous calls of parrots, a
fish eagle taking off like hope from the treetops into a perfect
sky, our steps deep in the gluey sand, the beating of my
heart, my fear, my prayer.

Yes, I did pray to those who have always helped. Who
have gone ahead where time means nothing, where anything
can happen. I prayed with an intensity which left a dry salty
taste in my mouth, tears stinging my eyes.

I prayed for the impossible to have occurred; for the
random, compassionate breath of Providence to defeat the
chronology of events, and to blow away, retrospectively,
the destructive fire; for the clouds to melt into rain and soak
the embers.

All the time I was thinking of the aeroplane, of the tanks
full of aviation fuel we had left below its wing, of our
breakfast fire that had seemed too close, that we had believed
extinguished; of the unbearable heat that the fire must have
caused . . . was it my imagination or was a blade of fine rain
falling ahead, obliquely . . . was it my imagination, or was
the smoke getting lighter? No longer like a leaden column,
but drifting wispily in the breeze?

The last mile was the longest. We reached the canal and

plunged in, partly swimming, partly wading up to our armpits. Then we came past the bend, and we saw it.

Up to our waists in the receding tide, Aidan and Mote, Mohamed, Ali and I watched, speechless.

Along the middle of the long strip of sand fringed with mangroves, several metres wide, half a mile long and beginning at the water's edge, was a dead stretch of burned grass, of charcoal stumps still glowing, like a grey carpet unrolled by that inferno. All the firewood we had accumulated below a thorn tree had been destroyed. A scorching, choking stench of smoke remained.

No more than two inches away from the smouldering ashes, on opposite sides, incongruous, intact as we had left them, were the airplane and our tent. Only one of the tent's strings was scorched and hung limp. In the distance, smoke still rose, some shrubs still glowing, but, inexplicably, the fire had subsided on its own.

Mote was the first to climb up the beach, where he fell to his knees, arms outstretched, praising Allah. In his way he voiced our own feelings: to the day we die none of us will forget that that morning at Rubu we had witnessed what we could only call a miracle.

I looked around at the baobabs, at the bush, at the sparkling sky. I looked down at the sand as I stepped from the water. It felt right and it was like an omen. There was a large lion track, fresh from the previous night, and a buffalo, I could see, had come down to the sea shore.

Night of the Lions

A brave man is always frightened three times by a lion:
when he first sees his track, when he first hears him roar
and when he first confronts him.

Somali Proverb, from *The Short Happy Life of Francis
Macomber* by ERNEST HEMINGWAY

It was the *askari* who brought Meave back in a wheelbarrow,
one April morning when I had been gardening.

The bougainvillaea were a riot of purple and needed
taming. The first long rains were just due to begin. It was
the right time.

I loved the concentration, which left my mind free to
wander, thoughts forming, stories unfolding, solutions finding shape. I liked the sun on my face and the sudden breeze
and the call of turaco from the treetops.

From the shade of the large yellow fever tree I saw the
strange procession approaching. Through the pepper trees,
in and out of sun blades, they came towards me. I stood,
putting down the secateurs I had been holding, and touched
the warm head of one of the dogs. There was a weird gloom
in the way they moved.

Dragging his long *kaputi** on the ground, his cap askew, preceded by two of the other dogs and followed by a gardener, Nyaga pushed a handcart from which the matted tail of Meave, caked with blood, trailed on the grass.

The dogs approached cautiously, sniffing with lifted noses, baffled. Meave was the oldest female of my Alsatians, the leader of the pack.

Nyaga looked up at me apologetically, his normally happy face split in a thousand wrinkles:

'*Pole. Ulipata yeye kandu ya bara bara. Aliona ndamu kwa nyayo: ni Simba. Uliona mugu.*' I am sorry. I found her on the side of the road. I had seen tracks of blood on the path. I saw the footprints. It's a lion.

Nothing I could do would save Meave.

She was alive; motionless; she looked up at me with a stoic acceptance of her fate, black eyes still, ears alert, impassive and fearless as Meave could be. I looked down at her twisted body, her hindquarters seemingly dead.

I had asked my cook Simon to bring a basin of warm water and ran to fetch my first-aid box.

I washed her gently and shaved her rump. She did not whimper, as if she had become insensitive to pain. And excruciating pain there must have been because, on the bluish skin my razor exposed, were four deep gashes from which blood still poured, round deep holes spaced like the fangs of a very large lion.

Flashes of the scene darted through my imagination. There were so many possibilities. Perhaps the dogs, out on their

---

* Military coat worn by night watchmen.

night's escapade, had found the lion on the kill. My dogs have learned that the lion's presence means meat to scavenge. They follow the feral scent through the bush early in the morning, before sunrise. They come back panting, wildness in their eyes and a rank smell on their fur, and jump into the fish pond exhausted, before drinking noisily from their bowls.

The story of their night's encounters, of meals shared with jackals, of bones fought over with hyena, the excitement of the hunt, will remain a mystery. I could imagine a short fight, the lion's annoyance, a deep growl . . . a snarl that becomes a bite, deep, deadly, effortless. A crunching sound of fractured bones. Like a rag, Meave flew in the air, landed in silence. The dogs scattered. The lion went on eating, unaffected. Meave's back was broken. She managed to drag herself a few metres away, below a *lelechwa* bush; and there the *askari* found her.

I disinfected her wounds with red mercurochrome which mixed with her blood, blotted them dry and stitched her thick skin with the curved needle from my kit. I applied powder and bandages, I did what I could: but I saw that her spine was broken, her back legs paralysed, and knew that the lion had won. I put her on a mat, in a quiet corner near my room where I could keep an eye on her; she drank some milk, but I could see that she was incontinent, and after two days she refused food and lay there with closed eyes, barely breathing.

It was a gun shot at sunrise, at the bottom of my garden. I had asked Aidan to help do what had to be done, but which I was incapable of facing.

She had been sedated with Nembutal and had fallen asleep, while I caressed her head. The echo resonated in the paling sky, startling the birds. A flight of starlings took off from the fever trees with a vibration of wings in the sudden silence.

It was a fresh dog grave next to many others, not far from the place where Paolo and Emanuele rest.

I went to look at the tracks that same morning and saw the lion's pug-marks in the dust. They were soft and rounded, immensely powerful and emanated danger.

Even more than a direct encounter, even before you hear his roar for the first time, it is the lion's footprint, marking the dust of a game trail, the unmistakable proof of his passing along the very path you are walking, that makes you feel that you are really in Africa.

After a time, living out in the African bush, you learn that there are animals you see and others whose presence you sense, not far from you, hidden by the undergrowth at the side of your track, the thick *lelechwa* or the clusters of euclea. Or in the night's shadows, expanding impenetrable out of your windows. In the border of darkness left outside your tent by the embers' glow of last night's campfire.

The elusive ones, whose scent only you detect, brought by a change of wind, betrayed by the cracking of a twig under a cautious paw. A powerful breathing, rasping and alien, rhythmic and implacable, like the very essence of Africa.

Those, the animals you never see, are the ones that give you the deepest shiver of emotion, the sharper taste of fear, the strongest longing. They are the ones you will remember. Like the nights of the lions.

Not so long ago, in January 1997, when Sveva was about to return to school in London, she asked me if she could spend at The Nest one of her last nights in Laikipia, before returning to Europe and the cold winter ahead. She hoped to see rhino. She would go on a night picnic organized by Shahar, our young agriculturalist from Israel, at the hot springs below the Retreat at Maji ya Nyoka, and would be dropped at The Nest, where I would fetch her next morning. She brought her sleeping-bag and her hurricane lamp and of course a torch. She would have a radio handset. She had done it before. But I was uncharacteristically uneasy, and went to bed, myself, with a handset radio resting on my pillow.

Even our cook Simon seemed doubtful tonight and looked at her seriously.

'*Makena*,' he pleaded, '*hapana sahau radio. Chunga sana.*' You, The One Who Smiles, do not forget your radio. Be very careful.

Lions had been roaring at night in Laikipia in recent days, more lions than I had heard in a very long time. At night I was often woken by my dogs' growls, by their rush of barking breathlessness as they ran for the door of my room where they slept, and were quickly lost in the night. They scattered on the lawn, howling high, as they felt the lion's presence on the hills. But when lions came close, the dogs kept quiet. They cowered back to my room and lay down on my carpet, with alert ears, unsleeping.

This night was no exception. The rhythmic deep growls

echoed on the hills on the side of the old Boma ya Taikunya, near the Ol Morani boundary line, and came closer. I could almost hear their padded feet on the track below Paolo's dam, along my garden, outside the guest rooms, as they moved towards the water trough of the *menanda*, where they could find buffalo, eland or zebra. I let the water overflow especially over the rim of the tank, where only elephant could reach it, so that it collects below it in a muddy hole, a delight for the buffalo. I suspected that lions and other carnivores had become increasingly attracted to the area. Landing one afternoon, I had seen a cheetah standing at the end of my airstrip, on an old anthill, checking out some young impala, undisturbed by the noise of the plane and swirls of dust; and at night I could often hear the magnified, see-saw purring of leopard: many impala went to the water.

I found it hard to sleep. Memories of danger haunted my mind. Still fresh was the memory of the recent encounter with the calf killer, in the last night of full moon.

When the moon rose I could see the cattle sitting around the *boma*, not far from the embers of the *wachungai*'s fire. They were mostly white, the cows of the breeding herd with their small calves next to them.

I was watching them through the thorny branches of the shrub I was sheltering under. My head covered in a cotton shawl rested on a double pillow, my blanket under my chin against the chill eastern wind. I was alert, and waiting. Next to me, stretched fully dressed on the mat, were Aidan with his lion rifle, Issak the headman with a spotlight and Ali the head of the *wachungai* at the *boma*.

The lion had come every night for the last two weeks, most nights taking off with one or two calves. The lion had developed a passion for newly-born calves. With any amount of young buffalo, fat zebra and tasty eland to feed upon, a lion addicted to killing cattle becomes a vermin no rancher can afford. Every week I had the cattle's *boma* moved out of the lion's territory. But the lion had followed, lured by the ease of taking tender young calves. Thirty calves had been taken, and I was left with no alternative.

Tonight, if the lion came, he would be shot.

He would come in the dark of the moon, at the time when the cold bites hardest, when the embers are greying and the men asleep. Wrapped in their *shukas*, curled around the camp fire, they would sleep without dreams until dawn, apart from the one keeping watch, fighting off sleep with scalding mugs of spiced tea, smoky with honey and milk.

The noise of cattle was in an odd way soothing, despite the snorting ruminant gurgles. The smell of fresh dung was overpowering, herby and natural in an odd way. I liked it.

I reflected that the smell had not changed in Africa over the centuries: no artificial fodder had been introduced to pollute the old ways. Cattle here lived outdoors all their lives; they wandered freely for their food and water; they were not stabled livestock, tame and safe in cosy enclosures where everything was available but freedom.

Here at the equator they got wet in the rain and walked for miles in the scorching sun to find water. They were resilient, patient animals, who knew how to survive; they recognized the song of the tick bird, the taste of new grass, they could smell a salt lick from great distances, and they knew lions.

It was as if a sudden wind had come from the *mukignei* shrubs in a short, intense burst; the same sound, like an immense, collective intake of breath. The cattle stood all at once, silent, alert, like weary ghosts.

And from the east, in stealthy, focused leaps, aiming straight for the youngest calf, came the lion.

Next to me, with astonishing speed, followed by Issak and Ali, Aidan had sprung to his feet, and while I kicked off the blanket, thankful for having kept my shoes on, and rushed for my gun, I heard the shot.

It shattered the night and echoed in the valley, with the deadly, disruptive finality of a rifle's burst. Deafened for an instant, running after the others in total silence, I heard only the drumming of my heart. A few metres away, in the dust the lion rolled, doubled up, gurgling its hollow death rattle. In a few seconds it lay still, and its eyes, no longer seeing, were a phosphorescent pale green, like dying fireflies.

Driving home later, alone at the light of the moon, trying to avoid potholes and hares on the rocky road, with the dead lion in the back of my car, I had wondered at the strange ways of my destiny and thought of other stories of lions in the night.

Sveva was alone at The Nest. The Nest is my refuge beside Ol ari Nyiro springs, a shelter of wood and stone open to suns and to moons, under a roof of thatched papyrus, with no windows or doors. It is built on a slope, overlooking a salt lick, and it holds a thousand spells.

There is the spell of the wind and that of the gentle rain. The spell of the storm, of thunder and lightning in the livid equator sky; the swallows' and swifts' spell, and the starlings' which roost on the beam above the four-poster bed made from old twisted olives and stones from the bush. At night come the fluttering bats with their special bat-spell of ancient caves, and dormice peer curious from their tiny holes, running fearlessly to pick up crumbs from my bread. Genet cats and porcupine come too, and leave their musky savannah spell, and in the night I try to guess which of them is chewing the remains of my guava. There is the spell that the orange-headed agama with the turquoise body laid on the stone under which Sveva's child hand had carved 'Paolo' and a heart of shells, and the powerful spell of the friendly cobra who sleeps underneath it.

There is the rhino spell and the elephant spell and the spell of the lone male eland. But the one that leaves me enthralled is Paolo's spell like a breath on my cheek, and Emanuele's, who had carved on to a log an acacia tree just like the one that one day would grow on his grave.

Presences of creatures and people like mysteries populated the shadows of my beloved Nest, but the strangest of all — and the one that kept me awake that night — was the one of the lion which sat on my bed.

A few weeks earlier I had visited The Nest with some guests, looking for buffalo. There had been a weird, sickening stench, the distinct feeling of a presence disturbed by our arrival, the glimpse, out of the corner of my eye, of a tawny shape dashing off down the slope, and in the sitting room, a large, evil reeking excrement, which I recognized for a lion's. Never before in Laikipia had a lion entered a house.

Narumbe, my wildlife ranger who was our escort that evening, had confirmed it:

'*Simba!*' he murmured, shaking his head in awe. '*Simba ndany ya nyumba!*' A lion in the house.

He turned his proud head round, still, like a wooden sculpture, flared nostrils sensing the wind, his perforated lobes, pendulous at the side of his head, alert to detect a revealing noise.

The Nest is built high on the hill, a perfect spot to survey the valley and watch wildlife. A few days earlier a young eland had been killed by a lion, just down below. Now, a herd of buffalo was emerging from the *lelechwa*.

'*Yeye natega mbogo hama siruai.*' He would be stalking buffalo or eland.

We had gone in, a sense of disquiet and unease. On the printed counterpane of my large four-poster bed, a fluff of coarse yellow hair confirmed the tale.

A lion on my bed. A lion on my bed, no one would ever believe it.

That episode, and the knowledge that animals mark their territory with dung and urine, had taken some of the shine from spending nights alone at The Nest, a place all open, impossible to lock, like a verandah. Sveva had shrugged off the eventuality of another feline visit:

'It will never happen again. Really improbable. We have disinfected and cleaned everything. His scent has disappeared. He would hate the smell of antiseptic.'

She was quite right. I did not give it another thought. Not until now.

Aware that Sveva was alone at The Nest, I was disturbed,

inexplicably alert and awake. I kept tossing on my pillow, resigned to a disturbed night of wakefulness.

The crackling of static that indicates that someone is fidgeting with the button of the radio microphone is as ominous as a phone ringing at night.

It started suddenly but hesitantly, and, although we have many radio sets on the ranch, I thought instantly of Sveva and was immediately awake.

'Who is at the radio?' I whispered in the microphone. 'Who is calling?'

It *was* Sveva. A faint murmur, tainted with fear and urgency.

'Mummy, there are lions. Lions. Close, very close. Help. Send a car quickly. Please help.'

I was out of the bed before she had finished talking, fumbling to get the lighter and light my candle. I grasped the torch, searched wildly for my glasses, dashed for the door, at the same time mumbling into the radio urgent encouragements and reassurances, suggestions of what to do.

'Take your hurricane lamp, ready to throw it if they come in, scare them off at the last moment, plan to startle them, do not panic, do not run. Whatever happens, do not run. It's going to be all right, I'm on my way.'

I was running. My heart beat in my mouth, I could not afford to lose time. I had run that corridor before, in a time of terror. In my nightdress, barefoot, I ran again on the bare stones, wet with night dew, over the wet cold grass, my dogs puzzled around me. I could still hear lion roaring down in the valley. The *askari* caught up with me as I fired the engine of the first car I reached, the large land cruiser we use for going around with the guests. I told him to stay near the radio in case I needed help.

'Simba!' I called out as the car moved off in a swirl of dust. '*Makena, na itua mimi. Simba na-ingia Nyumba ya Mukutan. Unaenda kusaidia.*' It is The One Who Smiles. A lion is getting into the hut on the Mukutan. I am going to help.

My voice sounded shrill, high-pitched, strangled. I was thinking about lions.

Lions are curious creatures, lazy, they fear practically nothing. In Laikipia I saw them countless times, mostly at dusk or returning home to Kuti at night, in my headlights. They stand, undaunted, in the middle of the tracks or beside them. They move away slowly with an easy muscular roll of the powerful shoulders, yellow and tawny, in and out of the undergrowth of sage bush and acacia shrubs. They sit down abruptly, with sudden abandon, attentive but not wary, yawning unhurried, never moving their inscrutable eyes from the car.

They often follow if I slow down, intrigued, unthreatening. But their indolence is never to be mistaken for friendliness, for wild lions are unpredictable to say the least. This is what I feared, their curiosity, the potent, careless, deadly playfulness of cats.

Never before were eight kilometres covered in less time. I was racing. Through the shrubs, into potholes, over stones and gullies. Up the hills, down the slopes. Zebra scattered. Then the *lelechwa* thickened, the track turned sharply left where an old twisted olive grew, the narrow trail climbed a rise, descended again: I was there. In the headlights my familiar Nest stood ghostly and grey like Dracula's castle in a Gothic tale. The wind blew sinister, sending shivers through the bleached wild sage. The night behind it held dangers and nameless threats. Where was my baby?

I hooted, frantically, with every blast of the horn scaring off my monsters. Sveva emerged tousled, frightened but intact, folding her sleeping-bag about her, holding out a tremulous hurricane lamp which looked so diminutive that, on second thought, no lion could possibly have been deterred by it.

She had, characteristically, recovered.

'So sorry, Mummy. It was horrible. He was so close I could have touched him. I didn't know what to do.' She gave me a half Makena-smile.

'How did you make it so quickly?'

She shook her hair. In her Paolo-blue eyes I noticed a sudden glint.

'But don't make so much noise. You'll scare the rhino.' I knew she was fine.

Memories gather in the night more easily, associations come naturally. It was when I was crossing the junction to the research camp, with Sveva sleepy in the car, that my thoughts went to another night, well over twenty years ago, more or less on that very same spot.

A story of other lions, in other times.

I had left Rocky and Colin Francombe's house – the managers in those days – with Emanuele, my mother and Gordon my dog. It was seven in the evening, dark already. It was the rainy season.

'Let's choose the middle track to Kuti,' I said to Emanuele. 'It is little used, mysterious, and there's more chance of

seeing wildlife there.' I looked up at the darkening sky:
'It may rain later. The road shouldn't be too wet.'

In upcountry Africa one lives out of doors, and one notices
the quality and the colours of the soil. There are endless
varieties, and in Laikipia one could find samples of most of
them. It is the yellow sandy dust of the savannah, or the
marvellous grainy orange murram of the Niuykundu Dam;
the fat, almost purple ochre of *mlima ndongo*; the brown
forest earth of Enghelesha, fertile with humus; the grey
volcanic gravel of the northern plains, and the light orange
or white powder leading to Mawe ya Paulo, which penetrates
everywhere, covering the leaves at the roadside with a sticky
film. And, of course, the feared black cotton soil of *damu ya
tope* and *maji ya faru*, which a shower of rain transforms into
a messy glue which clings to shoes and feet and tyres until
one gets hopelessly stuck.

There was a humidity in the air, a feeling of impending
clouds, but the night was still clear enough after the day's
downpour.

A buffalo crossed the track a few metres ahead, head high,
wet muzzle towards us, and stood there watching us unafraid.
I slowed down to avoid him.

'A big male. I must tell Paolo.'

His hind legs were encrusted with mud. The grey horns
spread wide, heavy, worn in the middle with deep ridges, a
sign of age. When the car was a few inches from him, almost
touching his hide, he shook his head and turned on his
hooves with the unexpected, lethal agility of old buffalo. In
seconds he was gone through the *lelechwa*, splashing long
spurts of brown mud.

The bottom of the ditch was flooded, and by now my car was too slow to negotiate the rise. Even in a four-wheel drive I felt the tyres struggling to grip the slippery bottom, skidding, burying deeper into the sticking clay at each burst of accelerator. It did not take me more than a few seconds to realize I could not get out until it dried out.

I went through the usual moves. Low ratio, reverse; I got out, wading in the mud and, helped by the others, put branches beneath the wheels; I tried again a few times but I was hopelessly stuck.

The light was fading fast. We had no radio. I quickly realized that Paolo, believing that we were having a drink with Colin and Rocky, would not think of looking for us for at least a couple of hours. Often Rocky would ask us to stay on for a bowl of soup and a glass of sherry and I would accept. Her cook Atipa boasted an endless repertoire of excellent soups, and I liked their company. Paolo would think we were having a good time. He might join us later. Only then would he realize that something had happened. In those days we had no internal radio network – and no way to communicate.

I looked up at the sky which was already dark, but with a luminescence at the horizon edge; I remembered that there would be an almost full moon tonight. The moon would rise in an hour, and even with the clouds there would be enough light to see my way back to Kuti. I would go with Gordon.

'I'm going to walk home; it's six kilometres from here to Kuti, I know my way; you stay where you are, keep each other company; I'll be back with Paolo in less than two hours. It will be fine. Cosy in the car.'

My words fell into silence. My mother looked at me, then at Emanuele. Nine years old, he was in Laikipia for half-term. He faced me, looking me straight in the eye, and even in the dark I sensed his determination.

'You are not going alone. I'm coming with you. Nonna can stay here.'

'If you go, I'm coming too.'

My mother sounded adamant. This was Africa after dark, a place full of wildlife. Perhaps she did not realize the danger or perhaps she did, only too well. My academic mother, used to museums and libraries, university lectures and hours writing at her desk in Venice. She did not want to miss out and had to be part of the adventure. If there was danger to face, she wanted to share it with us. I looked at her with new respect.

I argued for a few moments, but knew that I could not convince them to stay if they chose not to. Finally I surrendered. There was no time to lose.

'I will go ahead. You follow. Do not talk, do not make any noise. Stop if I stop. If anything comes too close don't run.' I looked at my mother's shoes and repeated: 'More than anything, do not run. Be quiet. Be still.'

I slid a pullover over my head. It would be cold. I nodded at Ema and moved on.

We were lighthearted to begin with, elated by the absurdity of the adventure. Gordon went ahead, sniffing, his tail erect like a banner. He turned to check on me now and again, came back to be patted on the nose, ran off again. Unlike the mad runs of our daytime walks, he kept close to us. We could still vaguely distinguish the silhouettes of the trees and the hills.

But I could sense my mother's justified concern and

Emanuele's excitement. I felt the responsibility, and a mixture of comfort at not being alone and worry at having to plan for three of us, should we have an encounter with something large and unfriendly.

The inhabitants of the night were about.

It is amazing how the silence of the night in Africa becomes quickly animated with presences and noises, as everywhere creatures wake up and take over; from the valleys they come, from the thickets of euclea and rhus, from the crags, the savannah and the plains. Around and ahead and behind us we become aware of creatures moving. And yet, in their presence they are silent, betrayed only by a deep breathing, a stomach gurgle, the swish of leaves opening and closing as a large shape passes through. Sometimes it is the elephant: a snapped branch falling, splintered by a strong proboscis. A far-away hyena, crying to the moon from the hills; a whining jackal's chorus, a lion's roar, the see-saw of the leopard; but mostly it is the tree frogs and the crickets and unknown insects singing incessantly in the background; and starlings when the moon is full.

So I walked, listening to the familiar sounds of the African night.

Sound of steps on cracking twigs. A disturbed guinea fowl getting excited in a burst of protest.

We followed the narrow road, little more than a track. I could just make it out. In places the bush on either side was impenetrable and too close for comfort. Then the bush opened out and I noticed a change in Gordon. He stopped abruptly in front of me, a paw in the air, ears pricked, listening; his nose had caught a scent; a low growl formed in his throat, and I stopped in my tracks; Emanuele and my mother stopped with me. Gordon moved his head to one side, still growling, as if he could see and smell what we could not. Then the scent was caught by a breeze and Gordon relaxed and moved again ahead. We followed warily.

I heard sounds of buffalo ahead, a large herd grazing; the distinct noise of many mouths crunching on strawy grass filled the darkness, belching and shuffling, stones rolling under heavy hooves, a warmth of many bodies and green manure. They blocked the way ahead and stretched in all directions. They surrounded us. Gordon took charge. He struck a pointing pose, rigid, and attacked the darkness.

We all stopped, braced for a stampede, which happened, blissfully, in the opposite direction. The night became rocks rolling, shrubs crashing, loud mooing and running buffalo. Soon only their warm, acrid smell remained.

At Kati Kati tank there were elephant drinking. I had anticipated this, and the danger of unknowingly cutting across the path of a herd of elephant or buffalo going to drink. Gordon was silent and circumspect, cautiously moving ahead. I knew the wind was on our side. We managed to move on unnoticed.

There were about two and a half kilometres to go; I felt relieved; but Gordon's behaviour had changed again; he did not walk ahead any more; he stayed close to my legs, as trained dogs do, a strange show of politeness; when I touched his head a few times I felt his tension and the hair stiffly risen on his back, like a hyena.

The night seemed much more silent than before; I could hear our steps magnified in this silence and felt exposed, very vulnerable, three generations of my family returning in the dark to our home in Africa.

Even the frogs and crickets had lost their voice. I found mine. To disperse the eerie feeling, I chose to break the rules. I started singing.

It was a song of snow and marching soldiers on desert sands and mountain tops, a song I had learned from my father as a child and that Emanuele had loved years ago, when I sang it to him as a lullaby. Soon he joined me.

> *Lungo le dune del deserto infinito,*
> *lungo le sponde accarezzate dal mar,*
> *oh quante volte insieme a te ho camminato,*
> *senza riposar.* *

My mother, now beyond bewilderment, sang with us too. A strange procession.

Finally we reached the spray race at Kuti and the familiar *menanda* looked ghostly in the moonlight; there were a few impala there. Startled at our appearance and uncertain whether to jump, they stood, fawn coloured and handsome, long-lashed beauties. Then suddenly they leaped high and fled into the night.

We entered the garden from the northern gate, and the other dogs ran to meet us, barking their welcome in a flurry of tails. We were safe.

---

* 'Along the dunes of the infinite desert/along the shores caressed by the sea/oh how often have I marched with you/without a pause of rest.'

Paolo, as expected, was reading in a room full of music, drinking his whisky on the rocks, and smoking like every night. When we came in, it took him a few moments to notice that we were covered in mud, still unchanged for dinner, with an air of excitement, like people who have just run a race and reached a goal. We told him the story and he laughed in approval. He would have done the same; he expected no less from me.

'Any encounters?' I told him of the buffalo, of the elephant. Of Gordon's sudden meekness, the silence of the night . . . he raised a brow, did not comment.

Next morning before breakfast he came towards me grinning. He took my hand and guided me out of the garden, along the path we had taken. There, very distinguishable in the drying clay, were our three tracks, my large ones, Emanuele's child feet, my mother's small prints; Gordon's paw marks following close to mine. And a few steps behind us, neat, all along the way, coming from a shrubbery after the middle tank, the rounded pug-prints of two very large lions.

'They followed you all the way, up to our gate.'

The tracks continued alone towards the bush.

PART TWO

Only Dust, at Arba Jahan

For Aidan, and to the memory
of Osman and of Ibrahim Ahmed

Oh, I could live with thee in the wilderness
Where human foot hath never won a way;
With thee, my city and my solitude
Light of my night, sweet rest from cares of day.

SIR RICHARD BURTON, *Wandering in West Africa*

Return to Moyale

Our camels sniff the evening, and are glad.

FLETCHER, *The Golden Road to Samarkand*

The airplane circled low over the tin roofs of the small frontier town built in Arabic style, headed towards the airstrip, and landed in a cloud of dust, hardly disturbing the camels. They looked up from the thorn-shrubs they had been browsing, totally unaffected. I noted how very white they were, like ghosts of camels.

It was a morning of September 1997. We had come to Moyale, in the extreme north of Kenya, on the frontier with Ethiopia. I was curious to return, for happy and poignant memories tied me to this remote and god-forsaken land.

The first time I visited Moyale was with Aidan, in 1990, in preparation for a camel trek. The purpose had been to make arrangements to purchase, and, the following year, to bring a herd of breeding Somali camels to the Laikipia region.

The itinerary would cover just over 300 miles across

Kenya's Northern Frontier district, from Moyale to a place called Lolokwe in Samburu district, next to the *lugga* of Il baa Okut, and eventually to Ol Penguan, Aidan's ranch in the savannah of the western Laikipia plateau.

For the first 200 miles, until the wells of Koiya, there would be no water. To take advantage of the cooler temperature of the night, the march was planned around the time of the full moon in September 1991. There were reasons for such a feat of endurance.

Aidan's passion for and understanding of camels was deep rooted. The original African livestock, adapted to the harshest conditions, to desolate places with scarce water, sparse forage and scorching heat, camels are far kinder to the ecology of the land than cattle. Their soft, padded feet do not erode the soil; they browse discriminately from tall shrubs beyond the reach of goats, thus never overgrazing the meagre pasture of Africa's most arid regions. Their dense, slightly sour milk is extremely nutritious and constitutes the largest part of the diet of most of the nomadic tribes of northern Kenya, whose lives completely depend on these animals. Unlike cattle, camels do not need to drink daily; they cover vast distances effortlessly, carry loads and are immensely adaptable.

It is clearly desirable to introduce camels in areas of Africa where they are not indigenous, but where conditions are suitable, as an environmentally friendly alternative to conventional livestock. They are also an attractive and decorative substitute for horses for tourist treks.

But a true passion is seldom born of reasoning; what most appealed to Aidan's noble, nomadic soul was the romantic aura surrounding these haughty, stately creatures, 'the ships of the desert', dignified, aristocratic, resilient, indispensable companions to any explorer of the Africa Unknown.

Another of Aidan's deep interests was collecting rare and often undescribed plant specimens, particularly bizarre subspecies of succulents like euphorbia, caraluma, aloe or aechinopsis, which still grow undiscovered in isolated, almost inaccessible gorges and peaks, weeks away from any beaten track. Most of his botanical expeditions would have been impossible without his camels.

When breeding livestock it is essential to periodically introduce new blood. This was the main reason for the scheme. The other one was, of course, the challenge of the difficulty, the beauty of the land, the danger of going through uncharted territory with just the basic essentials.

Purchasing dozens of camels, and in such a remote location, is a complex operation that cannot be accomplished in a few days, and much thought and planning went into organizing the expedition. Aidan was familiar with the procedure and knew the people without whom such a plan would have been impossible.

So I flew to Moyale with him, to meet his friend Haji Roba, an old dignitary quite prominent in that small Muslim community and a crucial figure in his plan. He would be entrusted with a substantial amount of cash. He would keep it in his rusty old safe, in the back room, cool with thick, whitewashed walls, separated from his front parlour by a yellow muslin curtain embroidered with red roses. He would hand out money over the following weeks and months to Aidan's man Ibrahim Mohamed, who was already on his way by road and would be based in Moyale for however long it would take to purchase a hundred camels.

Camels were brought to the market in Moyale from across the border, tall Ethiopian camels of illustrious breeding, the females good for milking, the males bred to walk tirelessly and carry loads. One day there would be five, another perhaps ten, and some other day none at all good enough to be purchased. They would be bought after long bargaining – the dealers sitting on mats strewn on the dusty gravel in the shade of an old tamarind, next to the *sokho* and not far from the mosque, just out of reach of the omnipresent goats – after drinking endless cups of tea with cardamom and comforting glasses of smoky-sweet *susha* curd.

It would be a man's world, in Muslim tradition, a world of business and trade, of caravans and mules, and talk of *shiftah*.

Shiftah.

Shiftah is the Somali name for 'bandits'. They are highway-men belonging to various ethnic clans, who continuously encroach from Ethiopia and Somalia to raid the borders of Kenya. They take advantage of the mountainous territory, inaccessible to administration, where they can easily disappear and escape capture.

Not a day would go by without *shiftah*-related incidents being reported: sometimes it would be only stealing a mob of camels, never without a lot of shooting, but in most cases there were serious casualties.

Shiftah would kill for livestock, but also for clothes, for shoes, for a watch, for the sake of killing. *Shiftah* were wild, brutal, unpredictable, and without mercy; often high on local drugs, they would raid *manyattas*, beat and rape women, slaughter children. They were not brave and gallant warriors, but bands of desperados with no honour, who, strong in numbers and weapons – they never attacked alone – would pounce on a solitary traveller and cut his throat for a few shillings' loot, or just because he belonged to the wrong clan. They would gallop in on fast horses, shouting and spraying bullets. *Shiftah* were no joke, and the only way to win was to stay clear of them.

Vehicles were no longer allowed to go on the murram road from Isiolo to Moyale without an armed police escort.

I remembered that first day in Moyale, and the secluded courtyard of our host, his lavish, generous hospitality, the shy beautiful little girl in the purple veil – his younger daughter, whose name was Rehema – slim and charming, with liquid, intelligent eyes, still little more than a child, who held a copy of the Koran, written in Arabic. She greeted me first by kissing my hand, then she moved to Aidan and lowered her head so that he could place his hand in sign of blessing; and when he did, she turned gently and gracefully kissed his hand before running back to the dark doorway, amongst the other scuttling small children. I noticed that now and again she raised her hand to her ear, twisting her neck, as if in pain.

To enter Haji Roba's house we climbed tall steps. In the shady room, we were greeted by some of his elder sons and, amid exclamations of welcome and commiseration for our long journey, made to sit on a long sofa upholstered in brown synthetic leather, before which was a coffee table covered in lace and adorned with a colourful arrangement of plastic flowers. From a charcoal brazier a pleasant resinous smoke of incense rose to the pale blue ceiling.

Soon the room was filled with other young men, other sons, and finally Mumina, his second wife, who was pregnant again, peeped from the door.

In the room with yellow cotton curtains, bright with bead-embroidered flowers, I waited for the time to pass, while the men spoke of their business.

Then it was time for breakfast – although it was more like lunch-time – and they showed me to a Turkish-type toilet built next to the kitchen where the women, squatting on the beaten earth floor, were deftly cooking delicious-smelling food on a small fire over three stones and singing.

A basin was brought, and a towel and a piece of soap, and we all washed our hands. Then platter after platter of food came, enamel dishes heaped with rice and goat stew and roast goat and goat entrails fried with onion; and *chapati* and lentils and banana fritters and sour camel milk with sugar and cardamom.

Ravenous, intrigued by foreign flavours, I ate more than I should have. Then Mumina came in and shyly embraced me, kissing me twice as is customary amongst Muslim women friends, and offered me a parcel, in which a fine Somali shawl was wrapped, red and yellow and white, woven of a very fine muslin. I draped it around my head and made a mental note to send back a present as soon as I could.

Haji Roba had organized for us to go into Ethiopia later for lunch, to meet a man who had heard of our arrival and wanted to meet Aidan. We boarded a rickety old Land-rover, borrowed from some merchant neighbour, and crossed the border without passport or any other document.

Everyone seemed to know Haji Roba; they waved at him from the side of the road and, to my amazement, quite a few people in that unfamiliar land greeted Aidan like an old friend.

We drove to a dilapidated hotel, squalidly decorated with rickety, cheap furniture, where we sat waiting for the man. He was the local government representative, a type of war-lord, quite high up in the country official politics. His name was Godana.

I looked at the hotel with curiosity since it was here, seven years earlier, that Aidan had been kept prisoner for a month, when, on a botanical expedition for the herbarium, having been dropped alone in the middle of nowhere by an airplane, he had been found by the local Garreh troops. Wandering the countryside with maps and compass in his rucksack, but no documents, he had been mistaken, with some logic, for a spy: no one could quite believe that all he wanted was to climb some unexplored mountain and collect rare plant specimens. *Wasungu* are all crazy.

Barely sustained by a monotonous diet of overcooked spaghetti of infamous quality, grainy coffee (dubious inherit-ance of Italian colonial days) and small bananas from a nearby grove, he was left there to ponder on his destiny, the door guarded by a sentinel who went with him even to the loo, until his rescue was organized.

Finally, the Ethiopian man arrived; with him came a polite, shy youth with eager eyes and sleeked-back hair, his son, Wako. So it transpired that university in the States was the young man's dream, an impossible dream, like journeying to a distant galaxy and we were the one bridge to that unknown. Feeling strongly for the boy, in subsequent months I did all I could to help. Years later the phone rang in Nairobi from the States, and there was Wako's jubilant voice, from far away, he who had made it after all.

We returned, making plans for the journey. Once the camels were purchased, we would fly in with Aidan's brother-in-law's airplane, a large, wonderfully old-fashioned de Havilland Beaver which could carry our bulky load. Our ambitious itinerary was dangerous, for the area was known to be riddled with *shiftah* bandits from Ethiopia. A large caravan with two Europeans would attract much attention, and we would have to avoid all known trails, and the crowded water holes for the first and major part of our trek to avoid being ambushed. The march was planned across dry savannah, deserts, lava stretches and seasonal swamps, with no roads or villages, and reachable only on foot. There would be no way of communicating once we had started our safari. The time of satellite telephones was yet to come. I would bring as comprehensive a first-aid kit as I could, and would hope for the best. With no refrigeration, there was no point in taking snake serum.

We would carry all the water we needed for drinking and cooking; we would wash only after reaching the wells of Koiya. Aidan would bring his rifle and the best camel men from his ranch: the two Ahmeds, distinguished with the nicknames of Nyukundu (red) and Nyeusi (black). I would bring two of my security rangers, with their guns, for protection. I would choose one who could speak the Adjuran language. We would employ some more camel handlers in Moyale.

Their leader would be Osman.

I heard that day, for the first time, his amazing story.

2

The Story of Osman

But one man loved the pilgrim soul in you,
And loved the sorrows of your changing face.

W. B. YEATS, *When You Are Old*

There was a little man who looked after camels, and his name was Osman Nguyu Dupa.

He was of slight build, with frail, bird-like bones but knobbly knees and large feet, like the animals he tended. He wore a long, cotton checkered *kikoi* and a loose turban, tied a few times around his grey hair, in the Boran style. He came from the Northern Frontier, close to Ethiopia, the land of sands and deserts, of lava rocks and unforgiving sun. His skin was dark and shiny, stretched over wide and prominent cheekbones on a haggard thin face with chiselled features, like the naïve black Christs painted on Coptic icons. His eyes were bright, mobile, used to scanning elusive horizons of trembling mirages for a sign of water, which means life; of endless dunes, for a sudden movement which may mean *shiftah*, and death.

His existence was of a biblical simplicity, timed to the camels' life and to their needs. Sunrise and sunset prayers began and ended every one of his days. He looked after the camels with brisk efficiency, singing to them, calling and herding them with his camel stick, walking tirelessly amongst them, behind them and ahead of them, by the end of the day covering easily ten times more miles than they had. He worked for Aidan as his head camel herdman.

Over the years they had shared many adventures. Safaris in the northern lands, walking for months through unexplored territories. They had shared star-studded skies in windy nights around the same campfire, and drunk from the same wells. Together they had risked their lives. Discovered once wandering illegally well into Ethiopia with their camels, Osman and Aidan had been taken prisoners by a local Garreh tribe, and held in their *manyatta* as spies. The local Ethiopian garrison, alerted by a runner, reached them on foot days later. After a summary trial under the scanty shade of the sparse thorn trees, they were finally freed. Small things, nuances, were responsible for their release: the women, maintained Aidan, had been instrumental in such leniency, appreciative of Aidan's help in lending the camels to help them carry their water from miles away; the men's curiosity about Aidan's rifle, and their gratitude for the penicillin he offered to cure the rampant venereal diseases.

A deep mutual respect had grown over the years between Osman and Aidan, rooted in the common love and under-standing of camels, the invaluable creatures without which no desert can be crossed on foot.

It was therefore with great dismay that Aidan realized one day that something was very wrong with Osman. He could not touch food, complained of a terrible pain in his stomach and seemed to lose weight almost by the minute. Finally, when he was reduced to a light bundle of skin and bones, Aidan had carried him in his arms to his airplane, and had flown him off to the Italian missionary doctors at the hospital in Wamba.

Wamba is in the territory of the Samburu, a landmark of eroded dry red earth scorched for miles around this extraordinary hospital in the middle of nowhere, where dedicated doctors minister daily to all imaginable diseases.

In the X-ray slide, an ugly, opaque mass occupied most of Osman's stomach. The tests confirmed that a malignant cancer in its final stages had expanded to extreme conditions, and that operating would be impossible. The kindest thing was for Osman to go back to his family and there to die there in peace.

One sunny morning, in a deep blue sky, Aidan flew him off to faraway Moyale, a corpse almost, and left him there in the shade of one of the rare thorn trees, his wife and children gathered around him in a silent circle, mourning already the inevitable loss. Alone over lava deserts, flying the long hours back to his ranch, Aidan felt with a heavy heart that he had seen the last of Osman.

Then, soon afterwards, Aidan heard news of a famous faith-healer who came periodically to visit terminally ill people in Gilgil, and of the amazing results of his ministrations.

In this land of the inexplicable, where most believe in magic, and where anything can happen, Aidan decided to give his old friend another chance. He booked an appointment, jumped into his plane, flew three hours due north, located the camel camp and Osman's *boma* from the air, circled twice and landed on the track in a cloud of white dust. Then, leaving behind a small bewildered crowd of people, camels and goats looking up in amazement from the remote strip of sand, he brought Osman in hope and glory back to Gilgil.

Again, he carried in his strong good arms his dying friend wrapped in a threadbare blanket.

It was a quiet, pleasant room with a few stools, a house plant or two, a table with a jug of milk, a pot of tea and some pink sugar-coated cake set on a tray. In the middle were placed a bench and a narrow bed. And there he laid him gently.

For many of the Africans, still unpolluted by western complexities, quaintly coexist, without conflicting, a total respect for their tribal witchcraft, and an almost unlimited faith in the capacity of European medicine to achieve the impossible.

Moreover Osman was a Muslim, a man of God, and there was in him a complete belief in Aidan's omnipotence: his companion of many adventures, the man who walked alone, who knew camels and could shoot straight, the kind, serious giant who was known to master the bird of metal with unparalleled skill, and had appeared from nowhere in the merciless northern sky to save him, was surrounded in people's tales, and in his heart, by an ineffable mystique. It was perfectly easy for him to accept that Aidan and the healer of the *musungu* God by the white hands would help him where everything else seemed to have failed. And it is on unquestioning trust and confidence that faith-healing is based.

They calmly explained to Osman what would happen. The doctor would put his hands on Osman's stomach, gently probing the swollen mass. Perhaps some heat would be felt. Perhaps nothing. Perhaps, if God was looking, the pain would ease, the evil ball would dissolve and Osman, if God wanted, would survive. *Inshallah.*

He was so weak that he was past caring. For weeks now his only food had been a few sips of camel milk, swallowed with difficulty. For months his constant companion had been an agony of pain. He had come to wish for an end to his misery, whatever this end might be. Death, the great forgiver, shrouded in white veils, would have been merciful. He closed his eyes, exhausted, dizzy with throbbing pain, ready for miracles.

The healing hands lightly touched Osman's tummy and a dry heat radiated all through it. How long it lasted he could not tell later; perhaps half an hour? But when the holy hands were lifted and the weary doctor wiped his forehead, Osman opened his eyes. He looked up and around, scanning the room with a new interest, focused hungrily on the dish of tea and the pink cake, pointed a bony finger and looked at Aidan.

'*Chai. Mimi nataka chai na sukari minghi. Na kipande ya keki, kubwa sana. Kwisha pona. Mimi ni sawa sasa. Allah Akbar.*' Tea. I want a cup of tea with lots of sugar; and a big piece of cake. I am cured. Allah is great.

He spoke with no surprise, accepting the inevitability of the miracle, Aidan's power, and the doctor's magic all at once.

The conventional doctors in Wamba were disconcerted.

The foul cancer mass was no longer visible. The X-rays were clear. Incredible as that might be, Osman had completely recovered.

They flew back to Moyale once more, this strange couple, the tall silent man in shorts and the small African in his *shuka*, landing again in the dust of the livestock trail. Again the children ran towards the shadow of the airplane, and, huddled together around the veiled tall woman who was their mother, waited in anxious silence for the plane to come to a halt skidding in the dust.

Even the cicadas had stopped singing.

The door opened, and in that silence Osman jumped out alone.

A collective intake of breath ran through the small crowd like the shiver of a sudden wind. Then the joyous whining began, the suffocated giggles, the lilting sing-song, the querulous talking all together.

'Get your strength back,' said Aidan in his farewell, 'and when you are fit again I'll send for you, and you must be ready. We will buy new tall Dogadia and Adjuran camels at the market in Moyale, and when we have enough I will return. You will come back with me to herd them. We'll walk them back together.'

As it happened, I walked them back too.

3

The Story of the Abagatha

He was a man, take him for all in all,
I shall not look upon his like again.

SHAKESPEARE, *Hamlet*

The pilot nodded to me and to John Wachira, the doctor
from A M R E F* with whom I was coming to visit the hospital.

'Here we are. I'll pick you up on Monday.'

So there I was, back in Moyale, looking forward to the
adventure. A different type of adventure from the last time
I was here. I had agreed to help the Flying Doctors of Africa
to raise awareness for their Outreach programme, and this
was a fact-finding mission to familiarize myself with what
was happening in the remote corners of Kenya where they
fly in regularly to administer all types of specialized surgery
and medical care, a daring, complex, romantic and desperately
needed undertaking. I would write a story for them. I would
stay in a hotel in the Ethiopian part of the town, and spend
the day at the hospital, where a room had been set apart for
me, so that I could write in peace.

*

*African Medical Research Foundation.

I stepped out of the plane and blinked in the harsh sunlight. The airstrip stretched dusty and unvisited; a shredded wind-sock hung limp for lack of any breeze. A few long-robed women, their heads covered in bright veils, stood on one side. Children came running, materializing from everywhere and nowhere. A Land-rover approached and people got out to greet us. Amongst them, I recognized Haji Roba. Tall and distinguished, a white Muslim cap on his head, khaki trousers, a coat and his stick. He came towards me smiling, holding my proffered hand in both of his, exuding genuine pleasure to see me. Having heard of my arrival, he wanted to find out if there was anything I needed. He asked me to go and have breakfast at his house next day, see again his wife, his children.

We drove off.

The town was as busy and dusty as I remembered, crowded with people moving in all directions and talking in excited, gesticulating groups. Slender ladies, clad in bracelets and muslin veils of red and blue and white, moved around, effortlessly balancing large bundles and enormous gourds on their heads. Goats foraged on heaps of old cabbage. Donkeys dozed wearily in the sun, and tall camels, tended by noisy leaders, ambled to the *sokho* carrying loads of merchandise from the Ethiopian side of the town. Dressed in flowing *kikois*, their bearded heads wrapped in *shammahs*, dignitaries conferred below the tamarind trees. The hot, still air smelled of dust and spices.

My return to Moyale was studded with novelty and unfor-gettable incidents, glimmers of another simpler and ancient world. I shall remember the hospital where young, bright

Doctor Mohamed attended to a hundred horrific emergencies with calm simplicity; the hopeful patients crowding the corridors like biblical figures in their casually elegant robes. The hotel where I slept in the Ethiopian town, a paw paw tree growing just outside my door, and huge cockroaches hiding under my bed. The eyes of the bossy little girl in charge of the shop where I purchased an embroidered white *shuka*, her sudden disarming smile when she said farewell in Italian. The young beggar with the gangrenous leg. The smell of the first sudden shower of rain on the dust, and the colourful market where, after much bargaining, I bought Sveva a red shawl. The woman pounding coffee grains with a long stick in a wooden pot, singing. The flavour of *gored gored*, the spiced stews, served in an array of *sufurias* set on the hospital floor outside the theatre at lunch time, when I joined the weary surgeon for a short break between operations. The muezzin's song from the mosque, merging with the prayers of the Coptic priest from the orthodox church.

But, mostly, the brief encounter with the Abagatha of the Borana, and the story of the *muganga* who cured Rehema.

Haji Roba disclosed that there was great anticipation amongst the Boran clan – a major proportion of the town's inhabitants – as news had come of the visit next day of their Abagatha. The Abagatha is the Boran's traditional leader, something between a tribal king and an elected president, and the highest authority of this noble tribe. He was sick, had heard of the flying doctor who had come to Moyale, and was being driven three hundred miles from their tribal domains to come and see him.

'Being driven?'

'Yes, the Ethiopian Government will give him a car,' revealed Haji Roba. 'The Abagatha of the Boran does not have his own vehicle. Boran ride horses.'

He explained to me about the Boran clan, to which he belonged. It is the largest Ethiopian clan, with several millions of people. They stretch from Ethiopia to Kenya and though they are citizens of the countries where they live, their ultimate loyalty is to their clan leader, the Abagatha. They follow their tribal law strictly, a fact acknowledged since the times of the British Colony, and accepted by the governments of the two countries.

The Borana are generally peaceful, but immensely powerful. Their traditions are deeply rooted. Their Abagatha is chosen from one of the families which have already produced other Abagatha, usually but not necessarily when still a child. He undergoes a complex education in their law, customs and secret, sacred ceremonies. He is recognized as the religious and political leader at the same time. He will be the Abagatha for eight years, when another trained youth will take his place.

Although most of them are now Muslim, traditionally Borana are neither Muslim nor Christian. They pray to God in the morning and to God in the evening, and have their rituals, but no specific place of worship. They can take as many wives as they choose. They are horsemen, warriors, livestock people, brave, gallant. Their Abagatha moves from camp to camp and so gets close to his tribe and their problems. His word is law, but he is known to be fair. He travels around with a retinue of advisers.

Naturally I was intrigued and extremely eager to meet this charismatic and mysterious character.

When we arrived at the hospital on the second day I knew instantly that the Abagatha was already there. An official-looking Land-rover with Ethiopian number plates was parked below a dusty palm tree, and groups of people stood expectantly at corners. From the silence and austerity prevailing I imagined that the patient would be a grand, dignified old man.

I was unprepared for the young person in long white robes and sandals, a type of round, rigid turban on his proud, handsome head with chiselled features, adorned by a lustrous beard. Obviously in pain, he sat on a bench and looked up at me searchingly with burning, intelligent black eyes. The ailment appeared to be an old calcified hydatic cyst in his liver, caused by a dangerous local parasite that becomes embedded in the body and grows into grotesque swellings, infiltrating every organ until the patient dies.

The medicines were not available at the hospital, and I offered to get them in Nairobi and dispatch them in the army airplane which brings supplies to Moyale every Wednesday. On learning this, the Abagatha sent an old man to tell me that he wanted to thank me personally. Soon he entered the small office they had given me, followed by all his escort, but without any special ceremony. He sat there on a narrow bench, communicating through an interpreter. He asked where I came from, and what was my occupation; he assumed I was a doctor, too, and looked at my computer with curiosity. On learning I was a farmer, he wanted to know if the rains had been good, if the grass was long and

Paolo loved archery

Sveva and Mote at Abukari

Kuki and Sveva and the dogs at Kuti

Paradise. View from The Nest

Sveva at The Nest on Ol ari Nyiro Springs

A pack of young lions in Ol ari Nyiro

The Road to Rubu: Tim and Sveva on a *bamba* coffee tree

The mangrove forest on the canal at Rubu

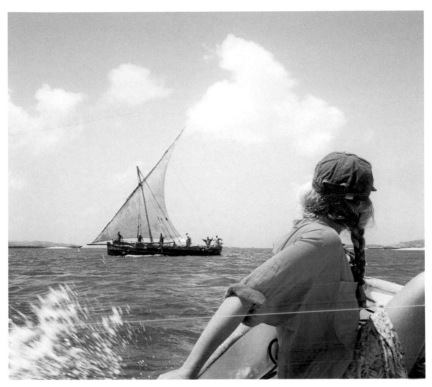

A daho off the Bajuni Islands and Sveva

Low tide at Ndoa

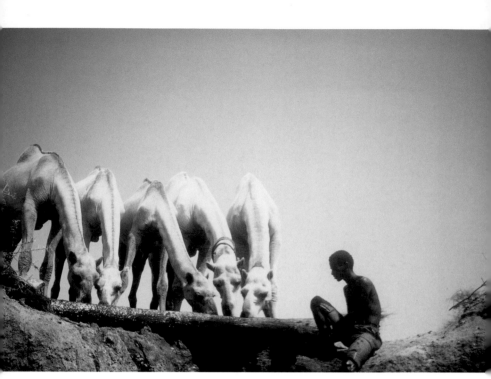

Ahmed Nyeusi at the wells at Koiya

Outspan at Matokole; twelve miles to Koiya

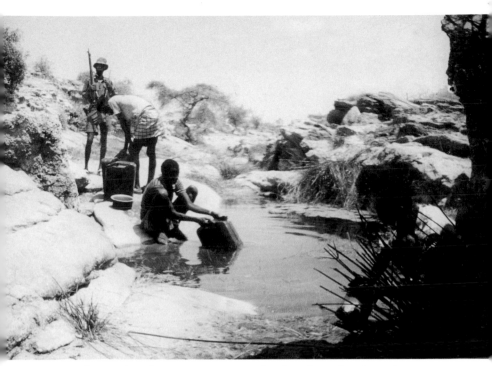

The pond at the springs at Lontopi; Ahmed Nyukundu and
Lwokignci Meto filling cans

The end of the safari

The acacia trees on the graves at Kuti

the grazing abundant, my camels fat and my cattle healthy; how many children I had. His penetrating eyes never left my face while the interpreter translated from Borana to Swahili. When he heard of Emanuele's death from snakebite he winced once.

From his concentrated gaze I could see something was puzzling him, and finally the most important question came, and it startled me. He wanted to know about my hair, which is quite long and streaked with blond. He explained that he had never seen hair which looked like a lion's mane before. Was it real hair? He moved a bony hand, its long sensitive fingers adorned by silver rings, to touch a lock on my forehead, and laughed suddenly, with white gleaming teeth like fresh matched almonds. I realized that I was possibly the first white woman he had ever seen, and certainly spoken to.

So it was that I was invited by the Abagatha of the Borana to be his guest, to stay at his camps, and share his food at his campfire, on the hills over the desert from where they can see the blue plains, where the nights are chilly and the days hot and dry; where they keep hundreds of horses, sleep in tents made of hides and time does not matter. I accepted immediately, of course. We shall decide on a date and this will be, I know, the ultimate adventure and another story to tell.

Haji Roba came back later that day as promised, to bring me first to the market – where, fiercely and jovially, he did all the bargaining on my behalf – and then to his house for breakfast.

I had brought a present for his wife Mumina, an ornate

golden thermos for her *chai*, incense sticks and a large box of sweets for his children.

In the internal courtyard I met his two new boys, all dressed in their lacy best clothes, who ran to greet me with lowered heads so I could put my hand on them in blessing, and a baby girl of a few months carried by a maid, all born to Mumina in the last six years. Mumina was older, rounder, but still graciously, maturely handsome, and the liquid, kind eyes glinted in welcome as she embraced me.

The house had not changed much. The curtains were now a pale green and the sofa covered with a synthetic type of leopard print. The walls were freshly varnished, deep green and white, and I noticed with surprise that the gold pendulum clock I had donated to one of Mumina's baby boys six years earlier, at the time of the camel trek, was still working, taking pride of place in the middle of a wall.

For breakfast I was served roast and boiled goat, fried rice, *chapati* and *samousas* and a good sponge cake with tea.

Haji Roba sat with me, eating sparsely with his hands, urging me to help myself, and narrating all the news of the past few years, slowly, with a wealth of details.

His adult sons had died. One had been ambushed by *shiftah* on the road to Isiolo. Everyone in the lorry was shot, including the armed escort. The other two were both wiped out during the epidemic of *dengi* fever in 1994.

As he spoke of heart-rending sorrows, of graves dug in the sand amongst the grey salt bushes, guarded by marabou storks, his genial face bore a mask of melancholy, and once again I marvelled at the acceptance of death of the African people.

And what became of Rehema? I had a vivid memory of the beautiful little girl who had served our food and could read the Koran, clearly a favourite child.

His face lit up and the wrinkles disappeared. Rehema was at a boarding school in Meru. She was doing well with her studies, and she had recovered physically, cured in the most curious of ways of the recurring ailment that had defeated all doctors, a chronic infection in her ear, which – as I would remember – had kept her in agony since childhood. Did I not know the story?

4

The Story of Rehema

For my part, I have ever believed, and I know that there
are witches.

SIR THOMAS BROWNE, *Oh Altitudo!*

After the last doctor in Nairobi, the Indian specialist at
the Aga Khan Hospital, declared that there was nothing he
could do to cure Rehema's ear, Haji Roba heard news of
a *muganga* from Ethiopia who could heal practically anything.

He was a wild fellow from the tribe of the Surma, uncouth
and untamed, with a savage reputation. He lived in primitive
conditions in a tent of uncured hides set in the bush, and never
wore clothes, an incomprehensible custom for a conservative
Muslim.

After much pondering, they finally sent for him, and when
Mumina saw this naked man with oiled limbs in her clean
parlour, she covered her face with her shawl, and immediately
dispatched a servant to buy some clothes for the *muganga*
to wear before she could meet him again.

The man took the clothes, spat on the floor, and wrapped
them around his dreadlocks in a bulky turban, remaining

naked, apart from the tiniest shred of material covering his genitals.

A reluctant, terrified Rehema was eventually brought to the room where the *muganga* crouched in a corner like an animal. He approached her, crawling, breathing noisily like a wild creature. He smelled her body from head to toe, stopping finally at the back of her head, still sniffing. Then he extracted some short sticks from his leather pouch and confirmed his diagnosis by passing them over her head and limbs. When the sticks began to vibrate, seemingly on their own, near her neck, behind her ear, there was no doubt. With a small knife the man made an incision behind Rehema's right ear which was, indeed, the one which hurt. Then he applied his big lips to the incision and started sucking. Poor, petrified Rehema cried and whimpered, trying to struggle away, but, undaunted, the man sucked and sucked, until – lo and behold – two squirming, white, fat worms wriggled out from the incision along with two small cockroaches which the man spat out in triumph, showing them to the revolted audience with a devilish grin.

I was disgusted. Haji Roba went on.

A goat was brought into the yard and slaughtered, her dark blood spilled on the dust like a prayer, and collected in a small gourd cured with ashes. The man smeared the still hot blood on his hair and face, and liberally doused the barely breathing Rehema. She was then, mercifully, sent to bed, where she tossed and cried for a few hours before falling into a fitful sleep, populated by the monsters of her nightmare.

When she woke up she was washed, more blood was

smudged all over her head, and the foul man again applied his greedy, obscene lips to her tender neck.

By now the man's mouth had been inspected by the entire family, scrubbed and rinsed with a toothbrush to ensure there could be no trick, until they were satisfied that it was empty. So, when another worm appeared and three more cockroaches were spat out in the basin, everyone caught their breath and prayed to Allah in awe and revulsion. Rehema was again sent to her room to sleep.

When she woke up next morning she was fresh and rested, the earache had gone and it never came back.

Haji Roba asked the *muganga* his price: ten Ethiopian birrs was all he asked, less than one English pound.

The man eventually returned to his wilderness, but not before Mumina's mother, an aunt and an array of sufferers had emerged to be cured. He extracted some hot, wet stones from a deformed foot, and some small snakes from someone's stomach, and disappeared in glory, naked as he had come.

Haji Roba adjusted his embroidered cap and smiled his crafty and humorous grin, and I never quite knew if he, a true Muslim, really believed the pagan ritual that he had described.

'*Rehema kwisha pona*,' he beamed, shrugging. Rehema is cured.

And this was all that mattered.

Haji Roba looked assessingly at me, and asked about the camels we had brought from Moyale in 1991, and how they were. Around my neck I still wore a small leather pouch he had given me all those years ago, which contained a page of the Koran, a priceless amulet to protect me during my travels. He shook his head a few times, shrugging off indulgently our European eccentricity, and told me that he had been quite impressed when he heard that we had actually made it, crossing the deserts on foot, avoiding *shiftah*, in such harsh conditions, because I was a woman, did not look that fit, and that journey was a true hardship and a thing for men only.

The camel journey had been a feat of perseverance, with no pauses for leisure, for washing, for resting. But the exhaustion brought by the long marches in the scorching sun; the dust, heat, swollen feet, blisters, sweat, thirst and ticks; the constant watch for predators and rustlers; the fear of losing the way; the fatigue of keeping up with the brisk, unrelenting pace of the camels; the worry for their safety, health and feed; the need to reach the watering wells within the limits of their and our endurance: all this had been tempered and made tolerable by the heady elation of moving through unbelievably beautiful, wild and unvisited country, and for me, by the awareness that such a rare and unrepeatable adventure was the fulfilment of a long cherished dream. I had, in my early twenties, been crippled in a tragic car accident. An invalid for a few years, unable to walk without crutches, I had dreamed of being able to march on healthy legs over the African savannah.

It had seemed impossible. It was happening now.

I wrote a diary of the trek every day, either at night by the light of the campfire or when we outspanned in the heat of the day beneath sparse, skeletal shades. It was an exercise

book bound in black cardboard, with curled up pages discoloured by sun and rain, in which I wrote in pencil.

It was still fresh in my memory. Before returning to
Moyale with the flying doctors I had read again the account
of that glorious, unforgettable journey, my journal of 1991.

And here it is.

But was there only dust, at Arba Jahan?

5

The Camel Trek

Where my caravan has rested
Flowers I leave you on the grass.

EDWARD TESCHEMACHER, *Where my caravan has rested*

Journal of a camel trek from Moyale to Lolokwe, via Il baa Okut: September/October 1991
with: Osman Nguyu Dupa, Ibrahim Mohamed, Ahmed Salat (Nyukundu), Ahmed Ibrahim Adan (Nyeusi), Mamhood, Gedi, Ibrahim Ahmed, Lwokignei Meto

Dololo Nure, 19 September 1991
Fujiyanyota – Dololo Chaka

The De Havilland Beaver flown by Tony Dyer landed at Kuti yesterday, at about 9.30 a.m.

We are ready.

Yesterday Aidan flew in late. He was still not completely well. The virus which has swept through Kenya and which has affected us both, has settled in my ear and affected his liver: what rotten luck. Because of this we had to delay our departure a couple of days, but we have finally resolved to go anyway, as everything is ready, our hearts are set on the adventure ahead, and we have to take advantage of the full moon.

We packed the night before to have all ready in the morning. As ever, I have more food than I can fit in the camel boxes. I have to rearrange tins and packets several times before I am satisfied, and much has to be left behind. Shame about the salmon and artichoke hearts, but I manage to smuggle in a chocolate dessert.

I bring two of my security rangers with me, a gun each, Ibrahim Ahmed and Lwokignei Meto. The latter is a young Turkana, while Ibrahim is of the Adjuran tribe, as are most of Aidan's camel people, and they know the main language of the areas we shall cross. We are unlikely to encounter anyone, but should we meet people we shall need interpreters.

So we take off on the bright blue morning of 19 September, bound for Moyale and our adventure.

Laikipia looks green from the air, but I know that leafy shrubs, streams and shady glades will soon become memories made of the substance of mirages.

We are bound for the desert.

We fly high over our itinerary: mighty and partially desolate from the air. Chains of mountains and dry *luggas*, open arid plains with not a sign of water, deserts, rocks of lava, the straight lines of abandoned oil-survey tracks, seemingly unending, diminished by a parched horizon of sand, dust and desiccated shrubs apparently empty of all forms of life.

Some ostriches and three oryx are all the animals I spot

from the air; camels, a few head of cattle – or perhaps goats – and limitless dunes and barren sands.

Dried out trees like bony skeletons, greyed by the sun.

Haji Roba expects us for lunch: he wants to give us a formal send-off in Muslim style. So I have to dress appropriately, with a skirt to cover my legs, while Aidan wears long trousers which had belonged to his father. I pack away my khakis and wear a new brick-red tricot ensemble, some jewels and a shawl. During the flight, engine oil spills on to me and stains my skirt.

Haji Roba is waiting at the landing strip, composed as ever, with a grin splitting his pleasant Boran face under the Muslim cap. We drive first a few miles in his rattling borrowed Land-rover to take our men and gear to join the rest of the team and the waiting camels.

From a clump of thorny shrubs filmed with white dust in the area where he has been guarding his camels for weeks now, emerges Osman; I have heard his story and I am eager to meet him. He is an exquisite old chap with a slim, wiry body and intelligent, mobile brown eyes. Quite short, but straight, and thin as only Somali can be. He looks fit and sprightly.

It is hard to believe that a few years back, this same man, reduced to a skeleton, was dying of advanced cancer of the stomach. He was cured by a faith healer and in a few days, he was back to look after his camels. The mission doctor, who had, with his own eyes, seen in the X-rays the lacerated remains of the stomach devoured by the spreading cancer, and left the moribund man to a sure grave, was rather shaken when he heard the news.

Otherwise, nobody made much of a fuss about it. As this is Africa where one accepts the inexplicable.

I like Osman instantly. Nimble, on crooked thin legs, he comes forward to shake my hand.

'Jambo, memsaabu.' He greets me in a flash of white teeth. I notice, startled, that he has the deep voice of a much taller man.

His liquid eyes scrutinize me attentively and I wonder if I have passed the test. The trek we are about to embark upon is a feat of endurance not really fit for a woman, an immense challenge. Two hundred and eighty miles without any water, in *shiftah* territory. Aidan, a former cripple, and eight men, one of whom is Osman.

Osman. After his amazing recovery, Aidan tells me, Osman bought a new young wife and went off to dig for gold in the Ethiopian hills. He found an insignificant amount of gold after several months and much labour; and when the danger dawned on him that he might be forcibly recruited into fighting the Eritrean insurrection to which he saw many of his companions being taken away in chains, he wisely went back to Moyale and to his camels, his true passion.

'Can you help me?' He points to his head, where I now see a long swollen cut, from which red thick blood is still oozing. He hit it on a sharp stump, trying to restrain a camel when all of them fled, startled by a hyena last night. Apart from two which haven't been seen again, all the camels have been found miraculously, taking advantage of the full moon.

The blood looks startlingly bright and shiny on his close

cropped hair, and I minister to him with hemostatic cotton from my first-aid box.

Haji Roba offers us the usual choice of roast and stewed goat, large bowls of steaming rice and meat, dates, *chapati*, bananas in chunks and, to drink, *susha*, the smoky yoghourt made with camel's milk, spices and sugar, cardamom tea and sodas. I choose a Coke, the last one for a long time.

I offer my gift of an ornate gilt clock to Haji Roba's young second wife Mumina, who has just given birth to a son. She embraces me warmly. My daughter Sveva has sent two glittery 'diamond and gold' bracelets to their eldest daughter Rehema, that delightful graceful little woman of a little girl, perhaps ten or eleven, who serves us with immense serious concentration, balancing plates on one hand like a dancer.

Haji Roba offers me his gift: a tiny leather pouch stitched by hand, which contains a page of the Holy Koran, a precious amulet to protect me on my travels; he looks me over pensively, as if trying to work out if I will make it, on foot, through the deserts.

We finally disengage ourselves from our warm hosts, and leave Tony at the Beaver, at the airstrip; it is rather late for his flight back to Timau.

As a parting gift Tony hands me two cartons of sun-dried raisins from his vineyards: the symbol of a European world so far removed from the reality we have chosen. He tips his hat, chivalrous as ever, climbs in and takes off in the dust while I hurry to change behind a malodorous, well-used outdoor loo.

Watching his airplane disappearing in the afternoon sun, I think that the last link with our world has now gone. We are on our own: we can only walk back over that forbidding torrid territory.

Ages before, when I was crippled in hospital, I had dreamed of just this: to be wandering in Africa, through savannah teeming with wildlife, with a romantic figure of a man – who belongs to that Africa – for my guide and companion. My dream of Africa had kept me going, yet I had no reason at all then to imagine that it would materialize.

I met this man when tragedy, upheaval and solitude prevailed; and now, in the ripe midday of my life, my physical wounds healed, but with more scars engraved in my soul, like the story of a surviving tree written with cuts and marks on its scorched bark – I am here, facing the challenge of the unknown.

I look at Aidan: his rugged face burned by many seasons of sun and rain; his noble head with its classic masculine features, his eyes of deep blue, familiar with deserts and mountains, prairies and drifting clouds; his long muscled legs and his slender figure made for effortless walking. He came into my life in days past, he went away and he has come back at my side.

That he asked me to join him in this adventure is a great honour to me: not only has he offered to share his solitude: he thinks I can make it.

Flying over the land we plan to walk through, I have some doubts: the landscapes look unforgiving, the distances immense. Will I be able to do it? Do I presume too much? Do I detect a doubt in Tony's eyes? Is the plan too ambitious? Even though my crippled leg healed long ago I am conscious that I have not regained total flexibility in my knee, and there are signs, almost twenty years after the final operation, that my leg is becoming shorter.

Whatever it is, I am taking a risk. I have now no option, and I am determined to try and live up to Aidan's expectations.

It is happening now.

I wear my clothes: new 'soft' (I thought! I was wrong) walking shoes, baggy trousers and a khaki shirt.

Our camels are waiting at Fujiyanyota, already laden by an efficient Osman, on whose head the hemostatic cotton has dried the blood, and sticks, startlingly yellow, like the feather of an exotic bird.

I admire the new camels. By the time of the full moon, Ibrahim managed to buy only eighty, not a hundred as we had hoped. Now seventy-eight remain: two escaped, when the hyena scattered them a few nights ago. Nine large impressive males, and a herd of superb looking young heifers, with dignified, graceful bearing, and startlingly white coats. I learn that this is Nature helping them to adapt to the extreme temperature. Darker coats would attract the sun, make the heat unbearable.

We leave Fujiyanyota about 5.30 p.m. Already a feeling of impending night in the reddening sky.

Ibrahim Ahmed cuts me a new camel stick from a special flexible shrub which grows at the side of the track. He de-barks it with easy strokes of his knife, and hands it over with a shy, chivalrous grin. I know that I will come to regard this stick as a friend. A camel stick to put across my shoulders, on which to hang my tiredness, clinging to it with dry hands, delivering to it all the weight of my upper body. A camel stick to love and to cherish.

We march and march, through sandy, parched country dotted with skeletal black bushes, along a deserted track.

Finally, I overtake the group of females.

I prefer walking ahead, with the feeling of choosing my own path, rather than following behind, trying to catch up with an ever advancing herd in the dust.

An hour or so after we start one of the pack camels walking in the rear, alarmed who knows by what infinitesimal disturbance, perhaps not used to carrying a load, bolts, a strap securing his load snaps, and his burden falls off.

The females, startled, go into a frenzied trot. I see them all bearing down on me, heads high, nostrils flaring. The earth trembles under their drumming hooves. Insecure about what is happening, I just dive for the surrounding thickets, to avoid being trampled.

The load is put back, with some labour; all the bundles have been scattered.

We go on and on, still fresh; the sun sets in a blood-red sky behind the spidery shrubs, and it is night. The moon is high, and casts a white-green light on the ghostly shapes.

A pungent, not unpleasant, dry smell of camel in dry country, dung, dust, aromatic plants. Strangely, I think, like the smell of raw tobacco.

Finally, my feet start aching. My knees and joints are painful, numb, unaccustomed to walking for hours without stopping for a moment – camels do not stop.

We walk for five hours without interruption. We outspan finally before a stretch of lava ('*bule*' in Swahili), at Dololo

Chaka. The men cut a *boma* of shrubs, built a fire, and we are each given a steamy mug of tea.

My legs feel like wooden posts, and the feet are agony. I fall exhausted on to my camel mattress, on which Aidan has spread a sheepskin. Looking at me with concern, he arranges a heavy blanket over me. I cover my head with a Somali shawl, drenched with aromatic sage oil to help my breathing, and sleep immediately, despite the chattering Somali.

I wake up with a pounding headache to a cold moon overhead. My watch says 1.30 a.m. I swallow two aspirins with water from my tin bottle, and manage to sleep only one hour before rising just after 4 a.m. Aidan is already up, and has gone to rouse the others.

20 *September 1991*
Dololo Chaka – Laga Mudama

We leave just after six. The sky is pink, the air still, heralding a hot day. It takes a long time to load the camels. The morning smells of resin and hidden things.

We walk on and on, following the track, passing a lava stretch and then a plain, then another long stretch of lava rocks. The road is dusty, with many tracks, mostly of hyena, Grant gazelle, giraffe, and many, many very large lion prints. I expect to see a lion any minute.

We outspan at 10 a.m. having walked for four hours. We have covered over twenty-two miles since 5 p.m. the day before – was it only yesterday? – in nine hours altogether.

Not a bad beginning.

Hot, dusty when we stop. So tired. Eat hot consommé, sardines straight from the tin and one orange.

Sleep a bit. Write the first part of my journal.

The place is Dololo Nure, under the hill of Kubi Maradab.

We leave again at 4.30 p.m.

Aidan rides for a time one of the pack camels.

My leg is aching.

We walk for four-and-a-half hours until 9 p.m., and outspan at a *lugga* called Laga Mudama. I eat an orange, drink almost a bottle of water, and sleep immediately, totally knocked out.

Garsa, *21 September 1991*
Laga Mudama – Choichuff

Wake at 5 a.m.

Slept very deeply. Headache. I guess I must get used to the heat and to marches without a pause. After my sedentary year at the desk, finishing my book, it will take a while. My leg is hurting. But I HAVE to make it. There is no going back, anyway, and I have dreamed so much of all this.

An orange. Water.

On our way at quarter to six in the morning.

Lovely overcast weather. After the first two hours I accept Aidan's suggestion and ride. Tall, tall that camel was. Comfortable, funny, undulating movement: I fall asleep twice. Wake up with a start, afraid of falling from my saddle.

Wonderful country dotted with trees. Cool and windy.

See two giraffe trotting along, Grant gazelle. Guinea fowls

and francolins everywhere, but too fast for Aidan to get them.

The idea is to shoot what we want to eat until we reach the dangerous *shiftah* country where a gunshot would advertise our presence. People have been killed up here for less than a watch. Our shoes, even, could cost us our lives.

Aidan walks ahead for four hours, carrying his gun across his shoulder. He looks very tired. The flu we both suffered from has taken its toll on him too.

It rains suddenly, bliss, soaking us to the bone with tiny penetrating needles of water. Letting the warm drops run down my face and licking the rain off my hands. Soaked in a few moments. The clothes dry on me in no time, leaving me refreshed.

We outspan at 10 a.m. after four hours' march, in a lovely greenish plain with trees, called Garsa, where I can now write my diary: how I would love to have the time to just leave the track, and S E E those trees, explore at leisure, stop in their shade, discover some secret creature and magic corners. Places we shall never again have the chance to pass through, and we cannot really say we have seen them at all, but gazed at them with desire from a distance. There is a pace to poetry, creativity and contemplation, and it must be harmony of body and soul. A restful quiet. A pause.

The slaves who built pyramids wrote no poems.

But I always knew that this was going to be no easy relaxed safari. This is a feat of endurance. Am I good enough, I wonder? I would hate to let Aidan down. He trusts me and has faith in my capacity to walk on for ever and to tolerate hardship. I must live up to his expectation. Damn the blisters.

Eat a heavy oxtail soup with onions made by Osman. Not the best cook this side of the equator, but he tries. Strange how hot food is welcome in the heat. Short vision of a chilled glass of white wine, the glass beaded with droplets, tinkling ice. No, we do not need it and I should not miss it.

Now, Aidan is asleep under an acacia tree.

I am enjoying this, actually. I have already grown to love and appreciate the camels.

The plain of Arba Jahan, 23 September 1991
Choichuff – Baji – Arba Jahan

(I did not write on 22 September; too tired.)
Off again on the afternoon of the 21st.

I walk, Aidan rides to start with. I suspect he does it to please me, so I do not feel that, when I do, I am being weak. He watches me. I know he is concerned about my bad leg.

I walk ahead grinding my teeth. Lovely country, and all the time we are accompanied by a haunting concert of whistling thorns. Eerie noise of the wind through the branches.

A few scattered Grant or Peter's gazelles; a flock of vulturine guinea fowls, necks adorned with blue feathers like lace collars, in the middle of the road track. HUGE lion spoor everywhere, hyena, honey badger, jackals and oryx tracks. An eagle-buzzard, huge, watching me from a dry tree stump; a deep blood-red sunset. Silence.

I walk ahead on the sand, glad to be here, proud of having dared.

Aidan insists that I ride and two hours later I accept.

My camel's name is Racub. A large mellow white Adjuran male. Rough saddle; hard; after the morning ride my legs are tender, my crotch painful. A strong breeze, kind to my burning face.

Curious, watching these patient, resilient camels from the top of one of them. Their strange, attentive eyes, long lashed, scrutinizing the soil they tread on with soft and gentle feet.

And miles of land unvisited and still, around and ahead.

At dusk we hit a lava patch, which goes on and on.

I have walked from 4 to 6 p.m. and end up riding until 10 p.m., for four hours.

Finally outspan just after this unending lava. We find an old *boma* in the dust, where we set our mattresses, too close to the camels snorting and chewing their cud, and to the people, talking around the fire.

A fierce moon, almost full on my face.

I do not sleep very well, but ravenously eat some delicious Italian tinned meat and pickled onions, welcome delicacy here at the equator.

On 22 September, today, we wake at 4.45 a.m.; still dark. Millions of jewelled stars. Smell of dust, camel dung, heat to come. We manage to leave at ten minutes to six, a record so far. An orange for my breakfast. Bless these oranges for as long as they last. Juicy, fresh, thirst-quenching. An orange is a luxury, a delight, a treasure to behold.

A lava stretch. Brown-black lava rocks, like burnished bronze, become almost red hot in the noon sun, burning through the soles of our shoes, a torment to the camels. Varied landscapes.

Soon, the round dark stones of lava give way to *acacia tortilis* country, soil of deep brown, with scattered limestone, startlingly white. The feeling of walking on a huge chocolate log studded with hazelnuts and almonds. Wildlife everywhere, and many tracks.

Peter's gazelles.

Two giraffe.

An oryx, like a cave painting.

Lion tracks.

Porcupine tracks, and scattered striped quills which I keep collecting and putting into my pocket, giggling all the way.

The resilience of these people.

Gedi and Mamhood, the kind Adjuran camel herders employed in Moyale, are tireless.

Gedi wears a loose, long checkered Somali *kikoi*, turquoise and blue, and a flowing white *shuka* on his shoulder. It is all he owns and he does not seem concerned. He is unconsciously attractive and naturally elegant like a camel or an antelope. The thought strikes me that nothing has changed in the look and clothes they wear, these Somali, since the time when the Three Kings from the Orient brought gifts of gold, incense and myrrh to the just-born Jesus of Nazareth.

Camel tracks, round, soft and gentle on the sand.

Having marched four and a quarter hours, I agree to ride again for three hours, and at 10 a.m. we outspan in the hottest place, Choichuff, and are instantly assaulted by ticks of all descriptions.

A very hot siesta; flies.

*

Ibrahim Ahmed damaged his nail, caught and crushed it while unloading, hanging red and yellow like a bloodied claw. I treat it to stop him from pulling it out there and then, the definitive solution he is ready to apply. It must be bloody painful as it is. I apply antibiotic cream, and wind a sterile stiff bandage around it to keep off the dirt. A strange sadness in Ibrahim's eyes even when he smiles.

'*Ah. Wewe doktary khabisa!*' (Oh, you are a real doctor), he praises me happily, the pain already seemingly overcome. They all appear impressed by my comprehensive supply of medicine and first aid.

They look good, my two Laikipia men, dressed in identical green shorts and military shirts, with their safari army gear and their guns. I notice that Lwokignei often asks Mamhood to carry his gun, but I prefer to ignore this unorthodoxy: in the middle of nowhere some rules can be relaxed, others must be kept firm.

If anything happened here, a serious wound, a terminal illness, a snake bite, there would be nothing or nobody to appeal to but our resourcefulness. No way of communicating with the rest of the world, and so far we have met not a soul.

We leave at 4.15 p.m. on September 22nd, still extremely hot. Aidan rides the first one and a half hours. My pillow is put beneath the saddle, which is now much more comfortable.

Blessed by a breeze.

I ride for three and a half hours, until 10 p.m., when we outspan on a dusty place in an area called Baji, a dry water hole.

Sitting in the dark next to the fire I take off my shoes and, looking at the blisters on my feet and the scratches and cuts that a few days of walking wild have engraved on my body, I think once again how much I have dreamed of this during the long months and years. I massage my leg where the long scars left by several operations remain. Aidan is watching:

'It is amazing that you can walk at all. That Swiss surgeon performed an absolute miracle. What was his name? Ah yes, Professor Müller. He would be proud of you if he could see you now.' He smiles at me. 'You should write to him; thank him; send him a photograph.'

'Professor Muller: I wonder where he is now . . . over twenty years ago . . . he may be dead.'

Aidan pokes the fire, adds a log, stretches comfortably on his mattress. He crosses his hands behind his head and looks up at the sky. His dark blue eyes seem almost black. His resemblance to Paolo strikes me once again.

'Tell me about him. I like to hear your stories.'

Holding a hot mug of soup, gathering a shawl about me, under a sky bejewelled with stars, listening to jackals far away, I close my eyes. From the treasure chest where my past sleeps, a face emerges, images of places long unvisited, train journeys, hospital smells, birds pecking at my window, the impression of a smile over a small moustache, twinkling brown eyes, strong hands, my bandaged leg. Hopes, fears, pain, trust . . . and memories unfold.

'Walk. Walk up and down the room.' There was a lilting authority in his strong accent, but kindness in his voice. 'No. Without crutches.'

He removed the long metal sticks I had grown used to

regarding as part of my anatomy. I looked at him appealingly: without crutches I felt vulnerable, inadequate.

'Walk.'

I limped like a lame duck, hobbling on the shorter leg, biting my lip in concentration. When I turned, he was frowning. Once more he held the X-rays against the light. He had of course already studied them carefully, before agreeing to see me. Complex cases intrigued him.

I realized that – like a sculptor who dreams of the statue he will mould from a mess of clay, or an architect planning a complex restoration of a damaged building – he knew exactly what he was going to achieve, what problems he could encounter, and how he would deal with them.

I looked at him with total confidence. He was my only remaining hope of ever walking normally again.

Professor Müller, the legendary orthopaedic surgeon in Bern, architect of miracles, was the best surgeon for the sort of fracture I had suffered in the tragic car crash in which Paolo's wife had died; the only one who could reverse the mess of past operations and heavy plasters that had gone wrong, who could repair my shrunken and crooked leg and make me walk again.

He looked at me intently.

'You'll need three, possibly four operations.'

He paused to see the effect his words had on me. I swallowed. After one year of plaster and two painful operations, four more operations, and the time in between, sounded like for ever. Like hell. I had been crippled for over a year now. The thought of more hospitals, exercises, anaesthetics, was unbearable. I said nothing.

He looked at me, cleared his throat.

'It can be done. It will not be easy. It will take time. You must help me. You are too young to be a cripple.'

Too young. I had just turned twenty-six, Emanuele was four years old, and I felt as if I was awakening from a long sleep to the possibility of being an invalid for life.

I simply could not afford not to be able to walk. There was Paolo. There was my dream. I wanted to live in Africa. Only that mattered. If it had to take four more operations, then so be it.

I looked back at him, and I managed to smile.

'Thank you,' was all I could say.

The lights overhead blinded me. I blinked. Already, the wave of numbness induced by the pre-anaesthesia was claiming me. I looked up. The kind, intelligent face smiled down on me. Brown, mobile eyes. The surgeon's mask hid his short dark moustache. He took my hand, squeezed it. I marvelled, vaguely, at the strength of that small hand.

'You will be all right. See?' The lilting Swiss accent in his polished French. He waved a sort of measuring tape. 'Your leg is going to be exactly of the same length as the other.'

The brown eyes twinkled. A needle in my arm.

'*Maintenant, contez avec moi. Jusqu'à six. Un, deux . . .*' I breathed deeply and repeated with him '. . . *trois, quatre, cinq . . .*' I never said six.

I woke up in my bed, a few hours of my life gone for ever from my consciousness. My leg felt heavy, loaded but not really painful.

My mother, who had come from Italy to help me, looked at me with concern.

'A much longer operation than he thought, he had to combine two in one. Four hours.'

The door of my room opened gently and he came in. Still dressed in his operating outfit, he marched to my bed. After the formal pomposity of the Italian dons, who arrived escorted by bowing assistants and a retinue of nurses, his simplicity took me by surprise.

'*Ma chère amie . . . ça va?* Stand up and show me how you walk.'

Incredulity, uncertainty, fear of falling. Standing and walking immediately after such an operation seemed impossible. He helped me up, fixed the drain from my wound to the belt of my hospital gown. He held my hand. I stood.

On the grey linoleum floor of that white-and-steel hospital room of the Lindenhof, with a dancing heart one afternoon of late July, I moved the first tentative step of my new life, no longer a cripple, the first step on my way to Africa. It would, one day, be the grassy plains of the savannah, the coral barrier of the Indian Ocean, the Great Rift Valley slopes, and now, the sand of remote deserts, the lava rocks of the North Frontier tracks. I owed much of my life to him. I blessed Professor Muller when I had to run fast from a wild beast, to climb a tree.

Professor Muller. I smile at Aidan. An extraordinary man, an inventor and a wizard. I wrote about him in my first book, just to thank him; I doubt if he ever read it. I wonder if he still works, if he is still alive. He seemed to me old then. I don't think I will ever see him again. It was all so long ago.

I lie down on my camel mattress, covered with a bed sheet and blanket. The sheet is a luxury which makes all the difference to my aching limbs.

The past is past, and this is my reality.

Far from the noise of the camels and the *boma* — thank you, Aidan — I spend the best night so far.

Wake up very early.

We manage to leave by 5.30, a record. Hot and very dusty track. I am determined to walk, the camels make me lazy.

Yesterday I made up many stories for my next book; I find this helps to distract me from the tiredness and weariness of walking in near silence for hours. Yesterday I imagined 'The Bull Shark of Vuma' and 'Fifty Guineas' Pike', and completed 'The Full Moon Island'. Would they ever be written? Am I creating a new book, here in these desert sands?

Today I did 'The story of Nungu Nungu'; as Aidan likes it and suggested I should write it, I shall dedicate it to him. I completed 'Emanuele's Chameleons', and I began in my head 'Only Dust at Arba Jahan'. This last one is prompted by the ever pervading dust. It could be the title of this safari's chronicle.

But how gently the camels walk. If they were cattle the cloud of dust from their hooves would be totally unbearable.

Long, long march, as we finally turn due south-west, on the long, unending desert track after Arba Jahan. We have to be careful to avoid the wells. *Shiftah* will be lurking there.

I admire Aidan's proficiency with his old brass compass, how he takes our bearings: it seems impossible that we shall ever get out of here.

We meet today the first man since we left, four days only — but they feel like four months, time has lost its meaning — a friendly camel herder of the Adjuran, sturdy-looking, carrying a curious leaf-pointed spear. He wants to sell us a camel, even on credit.

We outspan at the Arba Jahan plains, a windswept open area dotted with rare trees. Grassy straw. All the camels decide to come and feed from the tree we have chosen for our noon rest, one of two only, and far from each other, in a vast waterless plain. I am now writing here, having changed to a fresh blue caftan, closely observed by ruminating camels.

A blessed breeze: otherwise the heat would be unbearable. A few herds of camels file away in the heat waves and the distance, like mirages, silhouettes in a biblical scene; they must see us as we see them, but they make no move to approach us. They must be heading for the water hole at Arba Jahan, over ten miles due east, which we avoid as we have heard that it may well be dry, and full of desperate livestock, and starving Somali.

They will find only dust, at Arba Jahan.

Our valuable camels and our daring plan must be kept to ourselves. We do not want to advertise our presence. Ahead is *shiftah* territory.

This tree, a Salvadorensis, underneath which I am writing, is possibly one of the last trees for days. At this time, if he is not too exhausted, Aidan usually takes our bearings with his instruments and compass.

It is an old brass compass which I gave him, found in an antique shop in Nairobi, and which surely has a story of explorations in wild lands. I wonder where it has been and what were the eyes of the man who owned it like? What did he think, how did his voice sound, and was his woman fair?

Now, in the far distance, a ghostly evanescent mountain shape may be Marsabit. Aidan shows me a gaping void in the map, marked with lava symbols, a desert we must cross. I can see he is worried, he asks our people to fetch and load *kuni* on the camels, so that we can light a fire in the day – days? – to come, for our tea and their evening *posho*.

No trees mean no firewood ahead.

Dust, heat, thorns, a seemingly unending old livestock track, and finally the desert, lie beyond.

Just enough water to the wells of Koiya?

24 September 1991
Arba Jahan

We started walking at 4.30 p.m., yesterday afternoon, leaving behind the last yellow-grassed plains of Arba Jahan. Arba Jahan means 'Three Elephants', but there are no elephants left in the arid and cracked soil of this unwelcoming landscape. We have promised Tony Dyer to note any sign of elephant in our route, but so far we have seen none.

I like this place, however, its space, its silence, the feeling of walking on high land.

I am glad that we changed route. I feel like holding my head up and sniffing deeply, sensing the breeze, as the camels do.

Dark and dusty terrain, cracks covered in straw, full of

the white, conical shells of ground snails, which crawl in vast numbers out of their holes in the rains. Thousands of squirming, slimy snails. Revolting thought. I have always loathed snails.

We walk for two hours on the plains, where Aidan sees a cheetah with two cubs in the distance through his field glasses. But when I look, it has vanished. Mirages are part of the landscape here and encounters are glimpses, mysterious and evanescent, they escape long scrutiny.

I walk rather than ride, as I had in the morning, and feel in great shape.

At 6 p.m. Aidan shoots a Peter's gazelle, a young male, for the *watu*'s meal. A last treat before the desert.

It happens so fast. We spot a small group of gazelles in the distance, watching us with high necks, as still as statues. Without pausing a moment Aidan nods to me and gives me his hat to keep so that we can get on walking without changing pace, not to alarm the gazelles. There are about eight in a small herd, perhaps half a mile away. He pulls out his .22 without altering the rhythm of his step, quickly and precisely, with fluid movements, as a hunter must. We hear just one shot, quick as a whiplash. Then I see Osman leap high like a grasshopper and dash through the plains with a young hare's sprint towards the creature, to cut its throat as Muslim custom demands. Without this *halal** practice they cannot eat it.

Young Gedi, one of the two junior camel herders, runs

* Slaughtered according to the Koran rules.

after him with incredible speed, *shuka* flapping in the wind.

The horizon seems close and far away at the same time, and there they are profiled on it. I move towards them across the immensity of the plain.

The gazelle dies instantly, hit through the heart. Just enough time for Osman to slit its throat with Aidan's knife. They cut off its head, and in the dusty pupils, opaque and open in the twilight dusk, I can detect no pain. The memory of other dead dark eyes in the sun.

Jubilation, as meat equals a feast to all Africans. They throw the dead gazelle across the saddle of one of the pack camels and we move on.

We march and march for five hours through lava, and finally outspan at 9.45 p.m. in the middle of the track, the only possible place free of rocks.

A full moon, whining jackals and wild dogs and hyenas filling the night with prayers to the sky.

A lion roars at 12.30 p.m.

Wake up at 4.45 with an orange to wash my mouth of sleep, and leave before sunrise.

When the sun rises we watch it.

The desert lies ahead inexorable, forbidding, simmering in the distance. We cannot see its end. The sky is salmon pink. We stop a few moments to consider the challenge before beginning our march through it. Aidan turns up to me, our eyes meet and hold, and I nod. Just that.

'*Oho, galla,*' he prompts them. The camels snort and we move on.

I only walk for two and a half hours, my feet are aching

so much after last night's five-hour march and the five hours in the previous morning. I do not think I could have continued to walk this time. The heat is scorching. The lava rocks burn through the soles of my shoes like live coals; Aidan's shirt sticks to his back, its green colour already faded and discoloured.

I agree to ride. All the men are silent.

My camel's name is Racub; quiet fellow. I ride, with drizzling dreams, falling asleep in the saddle, for three and a half hours. Aidan walks, showing no sign of tiredness. This desert seems to stretch over the horizon for ever. The swelter lifting from the stones at noon is extraordinary. Heat waves like mirages of water tremble on the horizon, trees appear in the distance, dark, with promise of shade, but we can never reach them. They are illusions of the fever of the heat, substance of dreams or hallucinations.

The sides of the track are burned by some exhausted fire; ashes and carbonized tree stumps add to the inferno feeling. Surprisingly, strange oblong nests of invisible birds festoon the majority of the skeletal shrubs like hope, transforming them to ghostly Christmas trees.

Where are the birds I wonder, and what can they eat or drink? Not even insects can survive in this heat.

In my head I write 'The Secret Cove', a story of ocean, water and of long-lost days.

Driven by the fear of being held in that hell, we make it much faster than we thought: time loses any meaning when walking through endless, monotonous stretches of desert like this one.

We outspan finally in a god-forsaken lava stretch, after crossing another desert of burned grass and whistling thorns. The sun is high on the horizon, unforgiving.

The camels stand silently next to us, with bowed heads, without eating, searching for a sparse shadow, and elusive moisture. We make an illusory shelter, tying my green canvas *tandarua* to a low dried-out shrub and to the handles of our food boxes. We slide under it, no more than a foot or so, on the stained camel mattresses, and Aidan is suddenly asleep.

25 September 1991

I walk the first two hours, having left the desolate lava stretch at 4.20 p.m. I am getting used to walking.

The camels take a very fast trot, and the men sing and whistle in high spirits, galloping along as fast as them, and probing them now and then with their camel sticks.

Although I feel really well, I just cannot keep up and finally have to ride. It is a painful ride, as I am sore and hot.

Beautiful country, though, open, wild, with yellow grass.

Is the rest of the world still there?

Outspan at 10.30 p.m. on a pleasant enough open area, with tall dry grass.

The camels begin to suffer from thirst and too much heat. They are splendid creatures, and I am full of admiration and respect.

We are treated to the classic dish of liver, kidney from the gazelle and onions, cooked by Osman: but it is inedible, too salty, strong and gamy. A powerful after-taste of urea.

The men sing and laugh late into the night around their fire.

Outspan in the heat of noon below an acacia tree facing silent hills, live with wandering insects.

Leave this morning, 25 September 1991, at 5.10 a.m., having woken at 4 a.m. The camels doze nearby, nibbling from sparse shrubs in the stillness.

Aidan looks preoccupied while consulting his maps and searching the horizon for landmarks. A far chain of unknown hills is all we see. Where is water? Will we make it to it? Will the camels survive?

We have apparently taken the wrong track, and will have to cut across country, a thought I relish, as this will free us from the monotony of following a marked line, however faint.

But what if we get lost?

Aidan finally sights the lava ridge which is our landmark to Koiya and water.

We should reach it in two days, but I do not dare to hope it.

26 September 1991

Walk through much nicer land, seasonal swamps, not easy for camels as the dry shiny grey swamp-grass is slippery and hides some dangerous holes.

Aidan knows we have missed our track and is anxious about losing precious time, concerned about the difficult terrain ahead. Tall tangles of thorns and spiky shrubs reach the camels' shoulders and are practically impenetrable, dangerous as they could hide deep cavities and the camels could break a leg. Vicious little hooks dig scratches through our torn shirts.

But we must go ahead without delay. Water is the key. What will we do if we cannot find the wells? Aidan's mouth is set in a grim line. But I am in much better spirits, as the land-scape is so lovely and African and the pace much slower so I can easily walk. I secretly rejoice at our involuntary mistake.

Suddenly, on a straight stretch amidst tall acacia and thick silvery swamp grass, in a glade of afternoon light there stands a magnificent animal, unafraid and graceful, a male gerenuk. A fairy-elf of the savannah, who can only bring us luck. We watch each other for a while, then he leaves at his own pace, in elegant, unhurried leaps.

An unforgettable sight.

We leave the main track to cut across country. Luckily the landscape has changed, open now, with no more twisted shaggy bushes to impede the camels' progress: thanks, Eman-uele! I always appeal to him when I am in trouble. Aidan has been so worried that I have to cheer him up. I just know it will be all right. The camels patient, wise, gracefully bear their burden in long strides. My optimism is rewarded: a good lesson.

And then, in answer to my silent prayers and to make Aidan happy, we come to red sandy soil, dotted with acacia and comiphera. Totally wonderful walking through this terrain, resilient and solid soil allowing a bouncing step. My spirits lift as they have not in days. We outspan on a vast *mbogani* and light our own fire for the first time, while the men cut the usual *boma* of thorny bushes which will confine the camels for the night. Darkness falls on my happiness at having left the dreary straight line. The moon rises white and silent.

Then Aidan grimly announces that thirty camels are lost, and the herders are following them. They kept on by the light of the moon when we stopped, aiming towards far hills, which to them perhaps meant water. Like ghosts in the silvery light, they moved on, drawn by inexplicable instinct. There is nothing we can do but hope that our skilled people will catch up with them in time.

I try to cheer Aidan. If the herders can find the tracks by moonlight, they will follow them and we will wait here for a day. Not a bad thought, relaxing in this lovely country. Aidan is pessimistic. I reason that we are far from water holes and the confusing footprints of other camels, and that it will be easier for our skilled herders to follow the pale silvery tracks in the moonlight. But if the camels decide to go at a brisk trot, looking for water, it will be hard to catch up with them. They could be found by *shiftah* and stolen easily. It has happened before. And if the large lion whose footprints we detected on the track decides to ambush them, as is quite likely, they will gallop off in terror and we shall never see them again.

We go to bed early, having spilled the water, the salt, the muesli and the pasta!

But we underestimated our people; at about 10.45 p.m. we hear calls, whistles and screams. The night is full of activity. And we know they have found the camels.

*

We leave at sunrise on the 26th, happy, carefree, in excellent mood, through attractive pale yellow grass plains, rusty sandy soil. Compact and easy to walk on. Reach the lava boulders.

Outspan in a sandy *lugga*, under a clump of *Salvadoria* trees, a delightful refuge, and I feel happy. Ahmed offers me a special twig he has cut out of the tree's fibrous root, a valued original toothbrush to chew on. I am happy. Alive.

Aidan has learned the value of drinking water liberally during this safari, and although he is not at all well, he certainly has improved enormously. But he has blisters on his back, legs and his poor *sedere*. Bad suppurating tropical sores from scratches gone septic, which make walking painful with the chafing and the heat. I wash them with half a cup of warm water and apply antibiotic cream from my kit. I have convinced him to wear a loose *kikoi* rather than trousers, as our Somali do. He looks great in it, long-limbed as he is; and I feel in superb shape.

Matokole, 27 September 1991
Still twelve miles to Koiya

Last evening, having outspanned on a plain before dark, Aidan shot a francolin which we devoured, grilled on an open fire, impaled on a rough wooden spit, and spread with salt. A feast.

At bedtime, as I lower my head on to my mattress on the ground, I glimpse a quick movement, like a flutter, by my face. I have learned, after years of Africa, that instant reaction can save your life. Without thinking, I instantly sit up: a large pale yellow scorpion, the lethal *Sole Fugens*, disturbed by my gesture, his poison-laden tail arched, runs out of his stone, straight into the fire, where he sizzles to death in a few seconds.

We walk through the most beautiful country this morning: no sign of livestock or men because there is no water. But full of game. Grant – or Peter's – gazelles, oryx, giraffe, a landscape of tall fantastic acacia, open red-gold sands, a divine place. Walk for seven miles, between two lava ridges, of outstanding stark beauty. Must be wet seasonally, as there are signs of old livestock and MANY lion tracks.

Aidan tries to shoot some guinea fowl and francolins, but they are far too clever and fly off.

We take some photographs of the camels moving through acacia; then Aidan discovers that his camera has been empty all along! Tough luck. I have some good shots in mine, I hope. Now outspan on a sandy *lugga* of large acacia not far from Koiya. A disturbing feeling of people around. Although they are invisible, it seems that we can hear livestock bells.

The camels are all around me, lying in a circle and observing all we do. They nudge my head. They placidly guard me while I write. I wonder if they know how close water is: but is it?

Koiya, *28 September 1991*
KOIYA!!!!!!!!!!

Water at last, and TWO days ahead of schedule.

Clean, fresh, abundant, sweet water at Koiya.

We marched yesterday evening along a lovely, grand sandy *lugga*, Matokole: difficult walking, and I refined the skill of finding the hard bits of sand – usually a darker grey crust – on which to walk without sinking.

We meet four youngsters from the tribe of Rendille in bright beaded ornaments and red *shukas* — the first people, after that Adjuran herdsman. Then, their scrawny white cattle, in clouds of dust.

Lion tracks — these omnipresent but invisible lions — gerenuk, but incredibly attractive banks along the river, with trees and palms, huge acacia and enamel-green bushes. I wish we could stop below them, but we have to go on.

Instead, we spend the night on a small rise of white pebbles and grey soil; Aidan shoots two francolins in the *lugga* — and two for the men, who rush to cut their skinny throats — and we roast them on a basic spit on an open fire, a royal meal, plus half an orange each and hot cocoa.

Wake up at 11 p.m. with a fat tick stuck on my shoulder, gorged with my blood, little swine; amazingly, the first tick to bite me, in this tick-infested country, and we always sleeping on the camel mattress thrown on the bare soil.

Sleep soundly thereafter until 4.30.

Leave at 5.45 a.m. on the 28th September.

The camel bells tinkling away like birds in the noonday sun, we proceed, following countless livestock trails, all converging on this famous place, the only water in miles and miles, but the herds are always ahead and never to be met.

At 7 a.m. we come across a Rendille *boma*, tiny, with goats still crouching. A sleepy, cheeky young Rendille wrapped in a red *shuka* is milking them with lazy strokes, the sun already high, to Aidan's indignation. He cheerfully greets us with no curiosity as to how the hell we could materialize, two

Europeans and eight Africans carrying guns, with our seventy-eight camels, in the middle of nowhere.

Koiya appears at 8.15.

We stand for a time in silence, overwhelmed, to watch the target of our unforgiving progress.

A far outpost of the government. A group of *mabati* rondavels scattered on a rise, goats, a tiny *duka*, some round huts from whose dark doors people watch in silence. Luscious doum-palms on a *lugga* and clumps of tall acacia trees advertise the wells, like the oasis in the Sahara I remember visiting once with my father. That is it. We have made it to Koiya, after all.

From clumps of rounded dwellings that look like the yellow cocoons of giant insects, a thin figure in long robes comes to meet us, holding a ceremonial stick. He is a kind old fellow called Hassan, the councillor who – guess what! – knows our friends Jasper Evans and Maurizio Dioli, and buys camels for Jasper.

In Muslim tradition, he greets us with deference as weary travellers, and accords us the courtesy our status demands. In no time – and with some fuss – he organizes his well for us, and a secluded patch of trees to outspan under.

The well has been dug in the sand, the opening lined with round borders of a pale compacted clay, and the water is transparent and yellow like a topaz, incredibly inviting and, for me, forbidden.

The camels drink in disciplined shifts of four at a time, waiting patiently for their turn in the shade of the acacia, while we watch and the two Ahmeds sing the haunting Song of Water. This is an antique hypnotic tune of celebration, evocative and melodious, which is sung whenever camels are approaching water: for the camels it means drinking, and, obedient, they perform accordingly. If camels could laugh, the air would resonate with their nasal whines of jubilation.

I really admire the control and dignity of these creatures, thirsty as they are, who let their companions drink their fill before they move forward. They curve their gracious white necks and drink rhythmically, unhurriedly from the troughs carved out of hollowed tree trunks. Their caved-in stomachs inflate gradually before our eyes; the bony ribs disappear, and those haggard tired beasts are transformed once more into handsome, fit young camels ready to start the endless march again. They begin to feed instantly, peeling small leaves off branches with spongy lips.

Aidan buys our people a goat, assisted by Hassan who does the bargaining, and we shall feast on it tonight. Osman is busy frying oil in a pan.

Liver and kidneys and onions and rice will once again be our spartan/glorious meal.

Aidan goes up to his waist into the yellow tempting water, helping to fill the troughs, and I envy the men's freedom in the Muslim world which does not allow women to bathe at the wells, for fear of defiling them.

Now: the first bath in eight days any second, any amount of water, and I shall wash the dust off my hair, behind a charming screen Aidan is building for me, a perfect retreat, sheltered from people's eyes. Now and again he smiles at me. His beard has grown and gives him the patriarchal look of some biblical prophet.

I love him.

Torngong, 29 September 1991
Koiya – Torngong

We spend a blissful entire day and night at Koiya.

We set up our little den by a clump of trees, under a mosquito net, the first private and comfortable bed since we left. The men sing low and hoarse songs of love – of war? – around their fire.

Earlier I noticed, in an abandoned seasonal *manyatta*, curious contraptions of tall scaffolding made from branches; Aidan explains that they are suspended beds, to protect people from mosquito, which do not fly that high.

So I suspect the night will be disturbed, but in the event, not a single mosquito is heard. Too dry at this time of the year for them.

Soon after settling down and arranging our camping gear, the Rendille come with their amazingly skinny goats, but they soon pass on, discreet and unbothered by our presence, and Koiya is all for us.

I observe these goats and the most rachitic looking sheep, nibbling at invisible morsels of food, never lifting their patient, bent heads from the dust: they seem to eat just that dust, but Aidan informs me that in fact they feed on fallen acacia flowers, so small and inconspicuous as to be like powder. Extraordinary survival skills.

A girl comes over and I give her a sweet. She takes it shyly, runs away, and soon three more girls are there, waiting in silence. I give them a handful of peppermints each, and they go off together, giggling like tinkling bells.

*

I sleep, write, take it easy. Wash my hair and all my body, luxuriously, lazily and happily, with plenty of water. Change into a clean caftan; walk down to the wells to see the camels drink, and generally regain my human condition.

Leave at 5.45 a.m., having woken up at 4.30 a.m. after a disturbed night as the camels – too close – never stop thumping, and the men have forgotten to muffle the wooden camel bells with handfuls of hay.

Walk at a steady pace to the lovely hill of Sepi, boulders of quartz with trees in the smouldering heat.

I pour water, now fairly abundant in our jerricans, all over myself and my shirt and trousers, and I feel renewed. I am dry in a few minutes.

Soon on our way to reach . . . Kairu?

Now, on the evening of 30 September, sitting out on a plateau overlooking the hills. Hills like a stage, empty of actors. Close to an old *manyatta*. I write in the last light before dark, while the men are cutting a *boma* to enclose the camels. Lions are about and we could have a stampede.

30 September 1991
Torngong – Lontopi

Lions roared continuously last night at Torngong, very close to us, ready to attack; the night resonated with their hunting growls. The camels stayed awake, nervous in the dark, ready to stand and scatter in all directions. We had to build a stronger *boma* and the men slept in turns, with fires all around. I lay staring at the stars overhead, sensing danger, and sleep fled.

In the morning their pug tracks mark the dust around the *boma*. We leave at 5.50 a.m., and walk only three hours and a quarter. It is on this track that we find the first unmistakable footprints of *shiftah*: three people walking alone, with no livestock, wearing the characteristic rubber sandals, fashioned from old tyres, that they are known to favour. The men become quiet and wary. Aidan loads his rifle. We all keep looking around, uneasy at the silent, enigmatic hills approaching Lontopi.

Despite our concern, when we stop Aidan builds a shelter for me on the side of a reddish *lugga*, and I wash again with great relish while he keeps guard. My hair dries in minutes.

Lontopi, 1 October 1991

This is the idyllic place called Lontopi, in Samburu land where there are ponds among the rocks; where there are springs and palms and shady trees along the hills; where in the sun one can wash, and let emotion prevail.

On our way to Kairu, back on schedule now: not many miles – just over twenty – covered in the last two days, as the terrain is uneven and rocky and lion tracks are everywhere.

We shall now have to work hard, walk more, to keep up with our plan. But it was worth this rest and indulgence from 9 a.m., and the memory which will not fade.

These large camels, I observe, love to feed on the most improbable grey, desiccated weeds – *Indigophera Spinosa* – which must be powerfully nutritious, but look like cobweb.

I watch them nibbling at these frail delicate grasses with their prehensile lips, chewing them again and again patiently for hours to extract any nutriment they may have.

They munch away in great content all morning, and drink at the springs at Lontopi, while I watch them, perched on a rock like a baboon.

A beautiful mountain ahead, with great boulders and some doum-palms in the vast pink sand *lugga*.

Shiftah hide on these hills to survey the land around for their quarry. We could be that quarry, in fact. An eerie feeling, possibly being observed by cruel, invisible eyes, narrowed below lowered turbans. Images of cowboys in a Western movie being ambushed by impassive Apaches sitting on ponies from hilltops.

Everyone is alert and the men hold their guns carefully.

I try not to think of their AK47s and the long curved knives they use to cut their prisoners' throats. Osman, his eyes like slits, comes and talks to Aidan in hushed tones. They turn to look at me and I understand that I am the topic of their conversation.

The night is throbbing with crickets and strange unknown insects singing their diverse songs of life. I write by the light of my little diary cover, fitted out with battery and bulb, bought in a camping store one May morning in Washington DC, when I wore an Armani suit and had an appointment with a senator: days impossibly far removed from this reality. I notice that Osman has placed himself closer to us on my other side. Aidan is next to me, his loaded rifle at hand.

The night vibrates with tension.

I wake up early, stiff and covered in dew. I see Osman's

eyes on me, in the livid light before dawn, and know he has not slept.

I sit to finish my diary, while he revives the fire for tea.

For as long as I live I shall remember images of this unusual and unrepeatable safari – which has gone almost, already, in a soft haze of days. Places unvisited by man, reachable only on foot. Far from roads, miles and miles behind hills and *luggas* and waterless plains; lava hills and quartz sands, stones glittering with green and coral fire.

Patient camels, resilient, trustworthy, wise with the timeless instinct of survival in the harsh forbidding lands where they belong.

I shall remember oryx trotting off up hills, black tails flickering; the gerenuk surprised in the swamp, in the narrow path of grey silvery cane-grasses. The Song of Water at Koiya, exultant, melodious, and the jutting, darting walk of the wild Rendille warriors clad in red, with their fine faces and lithe bodies, muscular elves of the sand *luggas*; the starving goats and sheep searching for invisible particles of food amongst their own pellets; the gentle rhythm of the camel bells; the methodical unhurried chewing of their cud; their eyes, fringed with long wise eyelashes, their way of kneeling on the dust, sudden, complying. The funny shape of their sturdy tails, like huge silverfish; the way they urinate, backward, letting their brown gummy urine with its aromatic penetrating smell of unknown herbs trickle down their back legs to evaporate and cool them; the oily sap of the spicy *ginau*, the balsamic plant tasting of mango and turpentine; the colour of the rising sun in skies of red, the silhouettes of the camels against the horizon; the morning light on the pale yellow grass streaked with silver; the dust and twigs in the eye of the dead Peter's gazelle; a little natural shelter on the Arba Jahan plain, below a *Salvadorensis* tree, surrounded by the camels browsing on its leaves. The quest for Koiya and the elation, the sense of achievement, at reaching it ahead of time; the colour of the first water in the well, topaz yellow and transparent, so good to drink and fresh on my sunburned skin.

The Rendille girls, heads small, circled by bead ornaments, rusty red peplums over brown leather beaded skirts.

Our fires in the silence of the night.

The emotion of the pond at Lontopi.

The long ride on the endless desert.

Walking, step by step, in Aidan's tracks, the pattern of the soles of his shoes, familiar round marks on brown rubber.

The lion's roar with the moon. Its pug marks printed in the dust. Its feral smell brought by the breeze.

The ever present fear of invisible *shiftah*. The taste of adrenalin when we see their tracks.

Osman's eyes, coloured by his courage.

Tonight I am writing lying on the sheepskin on the camel mattress; the fire smoulders. A quiet intermittent touch of camel bells; songs of nocturnal insects. The sound of my breathing.

A breeze, like waves through the palm trees. The flavour of wonder.

Aidan, asleep at my side.

2 October 1991
Lontopi – Il baa Okut

At Il baa Okut, our second to last night in the bush.

Walk through Samburu land, across the Kairu *lugga*: huge expanse of white sand, doum-palms in large clusters and an almost dry well circled with tangles of thorns.

We meet two Samburu women and one donkey going for water. A biblical scene. Then a little boy in a red *shuka* herding surprisingly fat calves.

Hot, hot and very aching feet. Amazing views of the Ndoto mountains and Lolokwe in the distance, our target tomorrow, and the end of our journey, where Karanja will be waiting.

3 October 1991
Il baa Okut – Lolokwe

We walk along the pink quartz sand *lugga* of Il baa Okut, extraordinary old trees with hanging roots, on the banks among tall hills made of red granite boulders, emerging from a sea of green bushes. Osman walks ahead leading Racub, a youthful spring in his step. He turns to smile at me with true liking, and I am touched. I can well see why Aidan, who has been here before, so much loves this place.

The surprise of a lesser kudu, motionless, watching us from the middle of the *lugga*; a grey monkey, darting agile across, and up a tree.

Tracks of cattle ahead, but we never seem to reach them. I have grown to dislike cattle during this safari. Their total unsuitability to this land, and what they do to it: a lifeless, desolate landscape of dust and dried dung, flies, ticks, hoof marks and torn shrubs. The camels on the other hand, majestic and solemn, sail on disdainfully, leaving only their soft print, which does not raise dust, docile camels who know their names and people's voices, noble creatures. I am totally sold on camels this trip.

Now, waiting under a tree just before the rendezvous, where my driver Karanja should be already, with water, milk, *posho*, vegetables . . . but is not, so we send the two Ibrahims ahead to guide him here.

Aidan builds yet another bathroom for me, the last, the most charming of all, with my green screen and stones for the shower's floor, and I wash my hair, soap in bubbles, and I feel fresh, civilized. I wear a red caftan for happiness.

The camels are grazing quietly nearby, watched by those tireless herders, Gedi and Mamhood. Osman silently brings me a mug of sweet strong tea with ginger. We wait for the car from Laikipia.

We have today, at 10.45 a.m. completed 280 miles in thirteen days. Twenty miles a day average, though in the first six days of the safari we averaged twenty-seven miles a day; we slowed down when we stopped walking at night and left the track. It seems impossible to believe, but I actually made it.

The noise of an engine.

Karanja has arrived with my Toyota.

And this, then, is the end of the safari.

*

Later we send Karanja with Aidan's Samburu guide, and Ibrahim, to buy a goat in a nearby *manyatta* of Samburu Moran.

Tonight a last celebration. Then, Laikipia. The camels will proceed to Aidan's ranch with the staff: the remaining itinerary is not so intriguing, because it is not new to us, and we shall go ahead with the car. Karanja says there has been trouble with the government, and possibly Saturday there might be more unrest. It seems so far away and pointless.

4 October 1991

We feasted last night on the goat, with rice and fresh cabbage, and fresh milk with which I made Aidan a surprise treat of a chocolate mousse, having smuggled a packet in my saddle bag and saved it for the last meal.

Extraordinary how just a few hours of rest make one regain one's human condition, and the pleasure of appreciating the gift of wilderness. How one looks at things and savours them again. Our people have been great. Their prompt smiles, their hot teas, their morning songs.

Osman, a born leader, knowledgeable and wise, loyal to the end. Gedi and Mamhood, the two Ahmeds, Ibrahim and Lwokignei, my good Laikipia men, to whom I must give new watches as souvenirs of the trek. I do not think they have ever owned one.

Finished now. Yes, I am sorry it has ended so soon.

I only wish there had been more time, at least after Koiya, just to look around, to pause and perceive the magic of our surroundings. But the camels do not stop. One has to follow, otherwise one is quickly left behind. And camels are of course the only means of transport through desert lands, and the only chance to arrive here. So, there is no time to ponder on a bird or a tree, the gracious curve of a bank, a sudden view of hills and the shape of those oryx in the distance. An unhurried hurry is essential, inexorable and leaving no quarter. No chance to treasure the fleeing moment in the 'here and now', as the 'here and now' goes too fast, like a speeded-up film.

Like a marvellous book of complex and fine drawings, each leaf of which would be worth the pause of the attention, but the pages flick by too rapidly, without allowing the time to be observed, absorbed, and known.

Were it not for this scanty diary, scribbled in exhaustion in noons too hot for wisdom, in nights of distant jackals at the light of fading embers, perhaps I would not remember all the pauses, the views, some fugitive landscape already left behind by our unforgiving progress.

Yet I shall remember what I have not written too, as so complex and resourceful is the mind. And the colours and sounds and lights will come back unexpectedly years from now. I shall value these memories, and I know that when I am old and grey I shall look at my camel stick, shiny with wear, with deep nostalgia. And wherever I am, I will smell the resin and dust of the plains at Arba Jahan.

I am waiting for a welcome sound, the tinkling of his camel bell.

Isobel Burton, letter to Lady Paget

I turn the last page. There are other, more recent pages written in ink.

Laikipia, 30 November 1991

He survived the camel trek through lava deserts and we managed to avoid *shiftah* at the water holes, all the way up to Il baa Okut. We never met the bandits. But they caught him when he went home on leave, to rest. It was the time of the tribal clashes between the Dogadia and the Adjuran clans.

Shiftah ambushed Ibrahim Ahmed on his way to his *boma*, not so far from Moyale, and they slit his throat. I never saw him again.

They stole his new watch.

Laikipia, 24 December 1991

Aidan flew low over the house this morning and landed at Kuti before lunch.

'Can we take the car?' He smiled. 'There is something I would like you to see. Over the Corner Dam. I'll drive with you. Bring Sveva.'

We drive off in the late morning sun, leaving my house where the aroma of roast turkey and tortellini announces Christmas dinner. Even after twenty-five years, I never got used to a hot sunny Christmas, whose traditional tinsel decorations, made for grey snowy afternoons, look so totally out of place.

We meet a herd of impala and some zebra and eland and

elephant coming to water. But on reaching the last stretch of carissa shrubs I see them, and am totally caught unaware.

A grinning Osman, leaning on his camel stick; Gedi and Ahmed Nyeusi, smiling, loosened turbans on their proud heads held high; and behind them, the camels.

Tall graceful Adjuran female camels, led by Racub.

With a lump in my throat I turn to Aidan. I always thought those camels were for him.

'I had no idea . . .'

He is watching me. His serious, intent eyes hold a smile:

'The breeding females were always meant for you. And Racub. Sorry I can't wrap your present. Happy Christmas.'

He hands me an envelope. There is a card. A photo of myself at the wells at Koiya, with the camels drinking in the background in that blinding white light.

On the other side is written:

'Christmas 1991. For my love, fifty camels.'

Postscript

London, 15 March 1998

Osman, The End

One evening, in early February 1998, Osman Nguyu Dupa flew into Ol ari Nyiro with Aidan. He spent the night with Issak Ngolicha, our cattle headman, to whose clan he belonged and whose friend he was.

I saw him next morning at Kuti.

He had come to greet me. He carried a camel stick shiny and noble with wear. His traditional dress made him look taller: a long Somali *kikoi*, a shirt, a dark jacket, open sandals. A white turban of light cotton muslin was knotted a few times loosely round his head. I noticed that the hair showing beneath it was black, as if the grey I recalled had disappeared somehow, and he looked younger than I remembered him.

He was uncharacteristically cheerful, more talkative than ever before. He asked after Sveva, about what I was doing. I told him that I was completing a book – this book – and that the story of our camel trek of 1991 would be part of it.

He seemed extremely pleased.

He took my hand in his and shook it a few times vigorously:

'*Asante sana. Kukumbuka ni mzuri. Asante sana.*' Thank you, it is a good thing to remember.

He repeated this again with his deep, solemn voice. His serious, sorrowful eyes shone with a rare smile which spread over his ancient face with such luminous intensity that its memory still haunts me.

He was going on leave, to Moyale, for two months. Things were bad there. There had been lots of *shiftah* incidents in recent months. Many people had been murdered and a killer strain of malaria was rampant after the El Nino rains. All the same, he was looking forward to seeing his children. His teeth were startlingly white when he smiled.

It was the last time I saw Osman.

The news came to me from Aidan, one day in early March 1998, after sunset. He told me on the internal radio network, on the eve of my departure for London to visit my daughter and bring this manuscript.

Osman had been taken by *shiftah* and was believed dead.

The communications with Moyale were interrupted and telephones did not work. Because of the floods all roads were cut off. It was over ten days before one of my staff returned from leave with accurate news.

The Ethiopian clan of the Garreh has for some time been in the pay of the Tigre Government of Ethiopia, in order to report on the rebel Oromo clan, a related tribe, Borana-connected and speaking the same dialect. The Oromo rebels have been retaliating. Cattle and camel raids are the order of the day. People are killed. The Oromo *shiftah* have guns and knives and they know how to use them.

One morning, during Osman's leave, in full daylight, the

sky seemed to explode, detonating with screams and shots and cattle's and camels' cries. The Oromo *shiftah* were attacking the *manyatta* where Osman kept his livestock.

He was a few miles away and heard the commotion. Immediately he realized what was happening he ran to help. They tried to restrain him and failed. With him went a woman whose son, for whose safety she was concerned, was staying at the *boma*.

They were on the road to the *manyatta* when they were ambushed. The woman was savagely beaten and left for dead, and the *shiftah* dragged Osman with them to the hills.

There, they cut his throat.

News came of his severed arm, sent to the village as a warning of what would happen to others if they spied. The rest of his body was never found: no doubt it was left for the hyena that roam each night the barren Ethiopian hills.

At the time of writing, Aidan is flying to Moyale to find out more and to help and comfort his family.

When I return to Kenya, and we have obtained the necessary passes, we will go back together to look for Osman's remains. Almost certainly, it will be impossible to find them. But we owe it to Osman to try.

As a faithful Muslim, he must be buried with his head towards Mecca. Perhaps, this will be the time that I will call in my favour to the Abagatha of the Borana people. His support and protection will be invaluable in that harsh land, riddled with rebels, where human life has no value at all.

I shall write that account in due course. Now is the time to mourn. Sadness descends on us when we remember our companion in adventure, and reflect on the meaning of his violent and barbarous death. Our consolation is that Osman died bravely, and for one of his faith this represents certainty to be in the paradise of Allah, in the company of heroes.

As it is written.

London, March 1998

Glossary

Amani	Peace
Arufu	Smell
Askari	Night watchman
Ausiku	Night
Aya	Nanny, maid
Bahary	Sea
Bara bara	Road, track
Boma	Enclosure
Bule	Lava
Bunduki	Gun
Changaa	Strong, addictive, illegal local alcoholic brew
Chapati	Local pancake
Chui	Leopard
Daho	Wooden Arabic sailing boat
Damu	Blood
Debe	Can
Demu	Dam, pond, lake

Dengi	Deadly type of fever, similar to malaria
Duka	Local shop
Faru, kifaru	Rhinoceros
Galla	Camel, in Somali
Gamia	Camel, in Swahili
Gored gored	Ethiopian dish of raw meat
Habari?	What news?
Hapana	No
Inshallah	If God wills
Jabia	Traditional Arab method of gathering rainwater in underground tanks
Jambo	Hello
Jembe	Spade
Jua	Sun
Kaburi	Grave
Kanga	Local printed wrap for women
Kaputi	Coat
Kaskazi	Ocean breeze
Kesha	Tomorrow
Kifaru, faru	Rhinoceros
Kikoi	Local striped wrap for men
Kisima	Spring

Kufuata	To follow
Kuni	Firewood
Ku ona	To see
Lelechwa	Wild sage
Lugga	Small valley, ditch
Mabati	Corrugated iron
Maho	Small traditional wooden boat
Maji	Water
Makena	The One Who Smiles
Makuti	Thatch for roofing
Manyatta	Traditional living enclosure, Kraal
Mashua	Boat
Mawe	Rock
Mawingo	Clouds
Mbogani	Small clearing, small plain
Mbusi	Goat
Melango	Door, gap
Menanda	Cattle dip
Meno	Teeth
Mianzi	Bamboo
Miti	Tree
Mlima	Hill
Muchanga	Soil, sand
Muganga	Witch doctor
Mugu	Feet, tracks
Mugumu	Sacred fig tree
Mukignei	Evergreen shrub of euclea

Murram	Red Soil
Musungu, Wasungu	European(s)
Mutamayo	Wild olive
Mutandiko	Saddle
Mvua	Rain
Mzee	Old man
Nashukuru	I am grateful
Ndege	Bird, aeroplane
Ndofu	Elephant
Ndongo/Ndonga	Ochre
Ngombe	Cattle
Nyapara	Headman
Nyayo	Track
Nyeupe	White
Nyeusi	Black
Nyoka	Snake
Nyota	Stars
Nyukundu	Red
Nyumba	House
Panga	Machete
Posho	Maizemeal
Ringa	Slasher
Rondavel	Metal prefabricated octagonal huts
Rungu	Club, stick
Samaki ya mugu	Crayfish, fish with legs

Samousas	Local fried pasty with spiced meat or vegetable filling
Shamba	Small holding
Shammah	Traditional Arab man's headscarf
Shiftah	Bandits
Shuka	Wrap, shawl
Simba	Lion
Sokho	Open local market
Sufuria	Pot, pan
Tafa dali	Please
Tandarua	Tarpaulin
Tope	Mud
Wachungai	Cattle herders
Wasungu, Musungu	Europeans
Watu	People
Wazee	Elders, wise men

Samousas	Local fried pasty with spiced meat or vegetable filling
Shamba	Small holding
Shammah	Traditional Arab man's headscarf
Shiftah	Bandits
Shuka	Wrap, shawl
Simba	Lion
Sokho	Open local market
Sufuria	Pot, pan
Tafa dali	Please
Tandarua	Tarpaulin
Tope	Mud
Wachungai	Cattle herders
Wasungu, Musungu	Europeans
Watu	People
Wazee	Elders, wise men